BELIEVERS BAPTISM for CHILDREN of the CHURCH

BELIEVERS BAPTISM for CHILDREN of the CHURCH

Marlin Jeschke

Foreword by J. C. Wenger

HERALD PRESS
Scottdale, Pennsylvania
Kitchener, Ontario
1983

Library of Congress Cataloging in Publication Data

Jeschke, Marlin.
  Believers baptism for children of the church.

  Bibliography: p.
  1. Baptism. 2. Children—Religious life. 3. Infant
baptism. I. Title.
BV811.2.J47 1983   234'.1612   82-23406
ISBN 0-8361-3318-8

Scripture quotations are from the Revised Standard Version of the Bible,
copyrighted 1946, 1952, © 1971, 1973.

83 84 85 86 87 88 10 9 8 7 6 5 4 3 2 1

I dedicate this book
to my three children,
Eric, Margaret, and David.

Contents

Foreword

Reading this book has been a delight for me. One reason is that I myself suffered intensely as a teenager because I did not have the kind of conversion experience which Saul of Tarsus had. If only someone could have helped me to see that a "Timothy" had a devout childhood. It was easy for Timothy therefore to "cross over" from innocence to a declaration of sincere faith in Christ as Savior, and to the intention of making Christ the Lord of his life.

Marlin Jeschke has given us a thoughtful book, enriching the former treatments of Menno Simons (1539) and of Henrich Funck (1744). He makes us wince for too often glorifying the conversions of hardened sinners while not rejoicing adequately over the more gentle coming to faith of those brought up in the instruction and nurture of the Lord. The author helps us to see that in the New Testament era many of the baptisms were of adults who came to saving faith after having lived in sin for a time. Today, however, thousands of youth are baptized after a happy and largely carefree childhood of innocence. God's ideal is for this period of innocence to be the norm, and for making the crossover to saving faith—the appropriation of the faith in which one has been reared—at the first clear call of the Spirit.

Let no one assert that the writer does not believe in conversion. He does. But he urges the church to give more attention to happy Christian homes, to being more creative in the nurture of its youth, and to making baptism services occasions for joyful celebration. The whole process is *the more excellent way!*

Finally, this book examines the grounds of infant baptism honestly and patiently, with no throwing of bricks at pedobaptists. Yet it thoughtfully defends both a child-dedication service and the celebration of the coming to a personal faith in and loyalty to Christ by a meaningful service of water baptism. It is this believer's baptism which is most faithful to the New Testament symbolism of water baptism. This book deserves wide reading and earnest acceptance.

J. C. Wenger
Goshen Biblical Seminary
November 18, 1981

Author's Preface

Most people have alternating feelings about the subject of baptism and their experience of it. Baptism is usually considered a most important practice of the church; many Christians cherish memories of their own baptism. And yet the subject of baptism seldom if ever appears in their conversation, and they have a hard time generating enthusiasm for baptismal services in their congregation.

Until it comes to the baptism of their own children. Then baptism somehow becomes important again, though the usual lack of interest in it makes their children wonder why baptism has suddenly become significant.

Churches may profess baptism to be important, and of course they practice it regularly, but baptism is puzzlingly invisible on the public religious landscape. Evangelistic crusades may produce hundreds and even thousands of converts, but we never see these converts baptized, which should be considered quite strange in view of Peter's example on the day of Pentecost (as reported in Acts 2) and other New Testament examples. With few exceptions baptism receives no mention by radio and TV preachers.

The solution to this enigma is not hard to find. Baptism is a divisive subject, and if an evangelist introduced it he would be required to disclose his bias toward either infant baptism or adult baptism. In either case he would lose half his following—and if he vacillated on the subject, perhaps all of his following. Popular religious personalities have learned to remain discreetly silent about baptism.

There is also a somewhat puzzling neglect of the subject of baptism in Mennonite publishing. Believers baptism is usually held to be what triggered the Anabaptist movement when a small group engaged in rebaptisms in January of 1525 in Zurich. And although the affirmation of believers baptism is Article I of the Schleitheim Confession of 1527, yet there is a notable lack of interest in this subject in modern Mennonite literature.

Anabaptists and early Mennonites had a strong doctrine of baptism—indeed, of three baptisms: the baptism of the Spirit, the baptism in water, and the baptism in blood—the last usually viewed as the consequence of the first two. In early American Mennonite discussion writers were almost completely preoccupied with the mode of baptism. Mennonite writers sought valiantly to defend affusion against the pressure of their neighbors, the Dunkards (forebears of the Church of the Brethren), who championed immersion. Echoes of this polemic reverberated into the second half of the last century.

Otherwise, apart from a dissertation on Anabaptist baptism done by Rollin Armour, and a not widely enough known booklet on baptism in the New Testament written by Henry Poettcker, Mennonite publishing has not given baptism the attention its history would suggest it deserves.[1]

Numerous other writers, fortunately, have given the subject of baptism rather thorough discussion recently. After the respected theologian Karl Barth jolted the modern ecclesiastical world by declaring himself in favor of believers baptism, both pedobaptist and Baptist theologians returned to all aspects of the subject with impressive energy.[2] As a result our libraries now have a lot of good material on baptism in the New Testament, in church history, and in the modern world.[3] (The word pedobaptism comes from the same root as pediatrician and denotes the practice of infant baptism.)

In view of all the available and competent scholarship on baptism we do not need to rehearse all aspects of the subject here but can move on to tasks that still remain to be done.

To my thinking the biggest need in believers church doctrine and practice of baptism is making believers baptism meaningful to children of the church. Many thoughtful people in Mennonite churches have had a growing intuition that there is something wrong with a direct imposition of the New Testament model of baptism upon children of the church, though they hold even more reservations about traditional infant baptism. We need a theology of believers baptism for children of the church, and this book is an attempt to offer such a theology.

I recognize the risks in this venture, mainly the risk of inviting people to be willing to reexamine entrenched assumptions. It may sound presumptuous to suggest that the position here presented is new. No doubt intimations of it can be found in many places, but as a coherent whole I have not encountered it elsewhere.

This book is, then, an argument for a position. It basically assumes the believers church and believers baptism convictions and is addressed to readers of that tradition, though pedobaptists may listen in if they wish. While assuming believers baptism, this book suggests the need of recognizing the special and privileged position of children of the church and, therefore, of a proper adaptation of the New Testament model of baptism to their situation. There is something valid and important in what our pedobaptist friends have been saying, something we have not been willing to hear. To acknowledge it does not necessarily lead us, however, to pedobaptist conclusions.

But I can't say it all here in the introduction. For further elaboration of this thesis I invite the reader to continue in the following pages.

I would like to thank the many church groups and classes of students at Goshen College with whom I have tested the ideas presented here, especially the senior seminar of 1974-75, where I began this venture. Thanks also to my student assistant, Diane Diener, for her cheerful and efficient help and to J. C. Wenger for his encouragement in this project and for his Foreword.

The reader will notice that I speak frequently in this book of the "believers church" or of "believers baptism." These terms have become fairly common in recent theological writing to designate a distinct theological and ecclesiastical position in the way we have come to speak of Orthodox, Catholic, Reformed, and Evangelical traditions. To speak of the believers church does not imply that other churches do not have believers, just as to speak of Reformed churches does not imply that other churches (for example, the Anglican or Lutheran) are not reformed. Rather, the term "believers church" serves to identify a quite specific church type. (See James Leo Garrett, Jr., ed., *The Concept of the Believer's Church*, Herald Press, Scottdale, 1969, pp. 5-6; and Donald F. Durnbaugh, *The Believer's Church*, The Macmillan Company, New York, 1969, p. IX.)

In previous usage the term "believers" has usually been

written with an apostrophe, which tends to imply the possessive—that the church belongs to believers. To avoid this awkwardness Paul Jewett in his book, *Infant Baptism and the Covenant of Grace*, drops the apostrophe and speaks of "believer baptism," using the singular. I support this move and am merely returning to the plural, because community is of the essence of the believers church. The term "believers" is thus a straightforward adjective, not a possessive. Like the terms "Reformed" and "Orthodox," it designates a distinct type of church with a distinct type of baptism within the larger family of Christian churches.

Marlin Jeschke
Goshen, Indiana

BELIEVERS BAPTISM for CHILDREN of the CHURCH

Chapter 1

CROSSING OVER
Biblical Origins

Most Christians today tend to take baptism for granted, seldom reflecting on its origin and history. The phenomenon of baptism seems to break upon the scene of human history rather suddenly. The opening pages of the New Testament Gospels report rather abruptly the appearance of a certain John, called ever since "the Baptist," who stepped forward with the momentous announcement of the coming of the kingdom of God. "In those days came John the Baptist, preaching in the wilderness of Judea, 'Repent, for the kingdom of heaven is at hand' " (Mt. 3:1-2). The writers of the Gospels do not report John explaining, nor do they themselves pause to explain, the origin, development, and meaning of what appears to us to be a novel practice at the time. The interested reader of the Bible will look in vain for any immediate precedent for this rite or even for a reference to the term in the Old Testament. And yet John the Baptist and the Gospel writers seemed to assume that everyone around them understood the significance of baptism. By his actions as well as by his words John communicated something all Jews acquainted with Israel's heritage were expected to grasp.

Where did this rite of baptism come from? What did it mean? And what connection did it have with the appearance of God's kingdom? Although the New Testament does not offer us any straightforward explanation of the origin and meaning of baptism, we are given helpful information in rabbinic writings which, together with pertinent references in biblical thought, lead us in the direction of an answer.

Jewish Proselyte Baptism

At the time of Jesus, when much of Israel lived in dispersion, many Jews actively made proselytes. "When a person comes to you to be converted," says one rabbi, "do not reject him, but on the contrary, encourage him."[4] According to the *Encyclopedia Judaica,* "There is ample evidence of a widespread conversion to Judaism during the period of the Second Temple, ... and the word *ger,* which in biblical times meant a stranger, or an alien, became synonymous with a proselyte."[5]

Rabbinic instructions for receiving a proselyte called for an immersion basin, tank, or pool filled with about one hundred gallons of water. Into this the convert went naked in the presence of no fewer than three witnesses. While he underwent the rite of purification, teachers of the law accompanied the ritual with continued ethical instruction. In the case of women converts the witnesses were women. Nevertheless the rabbinic instruction still attended the ceremony through a curtained partition. It appears that the proselyte immersed himself without an administrant's hand upon him, although, as the presence of presiding officers indicates, the proselyte could not perform the rite by himself.

"A new name, usually from the Scriptures, was given during the act of baptism." Following the baptism the proselyte was considered "newborn," that is, as if he had been born of Jewish parentage. "His past, his country, his home and people [were] left behind.... The proselyte really began a new life."[6]

Proselyte baptism referred back to the exodus experiences of Israel in crossing the Red Sea and the Jordan in its deliverance from Egypt and entrance into the Promised Land. In these experiences Israel was cleansed, was brought under the lordship of Yahweh, and became a new community inheriting the promise of God. As Paul puts it, Israel was baptized in the cloud and in the sea (1 Cor. 10:2). According to rabbinic thought, "the Israelites were commanded to sanctify themselves before the deliverance of the law at Sinai.... The rabbis thus assumed that even at an early stage an ablution was the ordained means of gaining admission into the covenant." The proselyte was said to be brought "under the wings of the Divine Presence," an expression reflecting Israel's original experience in the exodus.[7] Thus converts to Judaism in effect belatedly reenacted Israel's exodus, vicariously sharing this experience of the Red Sea and Jordan, appropriating this history as their history and thereby becoming part of the covenant people produced by this historic event.

Proselyte baptism, though representing the act of individuals or small groups, and coming centuries after the exodus, nevertheless signified, like the original exodus, a deliverance and decisive crossing over from the pagan world. Such a crossing involved separation from the world and cleansing from its defilement. And it involved participation in God's new creation through acceptance of Israel's God, Israel's covenant faith, and Israel's ethical life.

There are those who would see the origin of baptism in the traditional Jewish purification rituals—the ablutions priests performed in the temple or the many purifications Pharisees practiced at the time of Jesus. Scholars point out that the Qumran Community of the Dead Sea Scrolls engaged in many and elaborate purification washings. But these are not likely the primary precedent and explanation for proselyte baptism, even though the purification motif doubtlessly surrounded every conversion and proselyte baptism. Whereas ritual washings were repeated, baptism was performed only once.

In our search for the origins of baptism we need not make the ceremonial washings and the exodus mutually exclusive antecedents. Purification rites and baptism both hold as their grand prototype the exodus crossing over in which God's people were created in the first place. The many ceremonial washings practiced in late Old Testament and New Testament Judaism intended to recall the significance of the exodus, no doubt as the practice of foot washing in the churches where this is observed today reminds Christians of their baptism.

For this reason we need not disparage all Jewish purification practices as perfunctory or as empty form, as many Christian writers have been too ready to do. Proselyte baptism could never signify merely ritual and ceremonial purification, for in the act of baptism the proselyte's motives were examined, and he was instructed in the law. Above all, for the Jewish community receiving him, his former idolatry, demon worship, and sexual immorality were no mere ceremonial or ritual lapses.[8] A proselyte's baptism marked a change of life. Pharisaic washings were similarly intended to be reminders of the seriousness of Judaism's break with the pagan world.

John the Baptist

The suggestion that exodus is the grand prototype of baptism is supported by the allusions and dramatic symbolism we find in the account of John the Baptist. John stationed himself in the wilderness at the Jordan, the point where Israel crossed over from the desert into the Promised Land, and John's action was intended to recall the wilderness theme of Israel's tradition.

The wilderness is where Israel as a people was born. God covenanted with his people at Sinai and continued to school them in obedience in the hardships of the desert. When Israel failed to believe God and murmured against him in the wilderness, he subjected the nation to forty additional years of desert wandering in order to purge the faithless generation and to raise up in their stead a believing and obedient people. " 'As I live,' says the Lord, '... your dead bodies shall fall in this wilderness; and of all your number, numbered from twenty years old and upward..., not one shall come into the land where I swore that I would make you dwell, except Caleb ... and Joshua ...' " (Num. 14:28-30).

Later, when Israel dwelt in the land but again repeatedly failed to trust God, the prophets returned to this wilderness theme, predicting a divine judgment that would carry Israel back into the wilderness for discipline and a new beginning. As Hosea puts it, "Therefore, behold, I will ... bring [Israel] into the wilderness, and speak tenderly to her.... And there she shall answer as in the days of her youth, as at the time when she came out of the land of Egypt" (Hos. 2:14-15). God would winnow his people, the prophets said; as a result some would perish, leaving only a remnant to begin a new chapter in God's purposes. "As I entered into judgment with your fathers in the wilderness of the land of Egypt, so I will enter into judgment with you, says the Lord God.... I will purge out the rebels from among you, and those who transgress against me; I will bring them out of the land where they sojourn, but they shall not enter the land of Israel" (Ezek. 20:36-38).

These prophetic predictions were largely fulfilled in the deportation and exile of Israel (around 587 BC). The land itself was in part turned into a wilderness. And in the forced march to Babylon and subsequent return of some exiles to the land, they literally traversed the wilderness. These dispersion experiences brought a major sifting. Many who were Jews only formally, by nationality or birth, abandoned their ancestral faith and became assimilated into the Gentile world. When Israel was thrown into the sea of nations, only those survived spiritually who in the absence of national and geographical identity possessed or found a faith as the people of God that distinguished them from the world and preserved them in their separate identity and life. It was from among those who clung to the faith that a contingent returned in 538 BC to reestablish a community in the land.

When John the Baptist launched his ministry with the announcement of the coming of the messianic era, he called for a symbolic return to the wilderness, even of those living in the land. He envisioned a momentous spiritual reentry on the scale of Israel's original experience in the exodus, covenant, and inheritance of the land. Somehow the original entry, and even the reentry from the exile, had not achieved the appropriation of God's promised blessing. What was needed was for Israel to return (which is what is meant by the Hebrew word for repent, *shub*) and to cross over not only physically and geographically, but in spirit and in truth.

John the Baptist seems to have taken the rite heretofore used to incorporate Gentile converts into the Jewish community and to have insisted upon applying it to Jews as well, implying that no one would be guaranteed entrance into the messianic order by virtue of descent from Abraham. All people stood in the same position in that they could enter the coming kingdom of God only through a personal act of return. John called the people back to that place in the wilderness at the Jordan where their forebears first entered the land, and he invited them literally, dramatically, and symbolically to cross over in spirit and in truth.

According to Matthew and Luke, the Baptist had special words of warning for those Jews who counted on lineal descent from Abraham for immunity from the coming judgment and for assurance of an inheritance in the coming kingdom. "Even now the axe is laid to the root of the trees; every tree therefore that does not bear good fruit is cut down and thrown into the fire" (Mt. 3:10).

These words would evoke in the Jewish mind those texts in the Old Testament describing Israel as God's planting, texts that predicted the wasting of vineyards or orchards that failed to produce the fruit of righteousness God sought. "I will tell you what I will do to my vineyard. . . . I will make it a waste. . . . For the vineyard of the Lord of hosts is the house of Israel. . . . And he looked for justice, but behold, bloodshed; for righteousness, but behold, a cry!" (Is. 5:5-7. Cf. Jer. 8:13-15). Jesus himself later referred to Israel in those terms in the parable of the fig tree. "A man had a fig tree . . . and he came seeking fruit on it and found none. And he said to the vinedresser . . . 'Cut it down; why should it use up the ground?' " (Lk. 13:6-7).

Preservation through the coming judgment and a share in the life of the new messianic age were not assured on the basis of Abrahamic descent, said John. "Do not presume to say to yourselves, 'We have Abraham as our father'; for I tell you,

God is able from these stones to raise up children to Abraham" (Mt. 3:9). Abraham couldn't see past natural possibilities when he tried, because of Sarah's sterility, to secure
offspring through Hagar to carry on the covenant line. But
God was not limited to the natural possibilities represented
by Ishmael. He was able to quicken dead generative powers
and provide for himself an Isaac, the channel he desired for
the transmission of covenant faith. John therefore advised
his Jewish listeners not to complacently assume status as
children of Abraham, for God is not limited to natural channels. He can bypass biological lineage if he needs to in order
to find responsive, believing stewards of the heritage of
faith.

Many Jews rightly considered themselves descendants of
Abraham; they took seriously God's promise to him: "I will
establish my covenant between me and you and your
descendants after you throughout their generations for an
everlasting covenant" (Gen. 17:7). Nonetheless, a twofold
movement developed over the centuries of Jewish history:
on the one hand, the apostasy and reprobation of lineal
descendants of Abraham; and on the other, the conversion
and accession of Gentiles to the covenant community. Let us
trace this double movement briefly.

Every literate Jew would know the story of Abraham very
well. Of Abraham's two sons, Ishmael and Isaac, God found
only Isaac worthy to inherit the covenant. And of Isaac's two
sons, Esau and Jacob, only Jacob inherited the covenant
blessing, because Esau despised his birthright. In each of
these cases the transmission of faith went in other than the
ordinary, traditional, even culturally "proper" and humanly
expected channels. Already in the third generation only a
small fraction of the natural descendants of Abraham could
be included in the community of faith, the fraction,

moreover, one would least expect to find there, naturally speaking. Since Jews took the stories of the patriarchs to be most instructive as prototypes of faith and obedience, this could not but represent a serious object lesson about divine election and human faith.

Of the descendants of Jacob who fell into bondage in Egypt but were delivered by God's mighty hand, not all made it into the Promised Land. Over the centuries many others doubtless forsook their ancestral faith, though not in wholesale lots, not necessarily in times of crisis such as the wilderness or deportation, and perhaps for a wide variety of reasons—intermarriage, economic advancement, and acculturation into the Gentile world.

Over against this spiritual attrition of Abraham's faithful descendants, we find a counter movement of accession of Gentiles to Hebrew faith through conversion. Already at the time of the exodus of Israel from Egypt "a mixed multitude also went up with them," we are told (Ex. 12:38). The people that met God at Sinai and accepted the covenant under Moses apparently included some non-Hebrews who were not descendants of Jacob. And over the centuries there were people such as Rahab and Ruth, Uriah the Hittite, and wives of King David who got incorporated into the community of Israel. As we have already noted, at the time of Jesus not only did the doors of Judaism stand open for the reception of Gentile converts, but Jews engaged in active missionizing. (Such proselytization later ceased mainly because of Byzantine laws forbidding it under penalty of death.)

We see, then, a double movement in Israel's history: On the one hand, many Jews could and did abandon Israel's faith and lose their inheritance in the covenant community. Gentiles, on the other hand, had the opportunity to appropriate Israel's faith and to share with the seed of Abraham the blessings of the covenant. Long before Paul said it in Galatians, it was obvious that "it is men of faith who are the sons of Abraham" (Gal. 3:7), even though this lineage of faith did coincide to a great extent with biological descent—and properly so. Children of believers have always had the best exposure to the appeal of the covenant of faith. At the same time *the double movement of apostasy and conversion, of attrition and accession, demonstrates a "believers church" principle operative already throughout the history of Israel, from Abraham to John the Baptist.* This is so even if Israel continued to be regarded by itself and others as an ethnic community consisting of the lineal descendants of Abraham.

These two conceptions of Israel—ethnic nation versus community of faith—came into uneasy tension already long before the rise of the Christian movement. As early as the time of the prophets the vision had been presented of a new day, a messianic age, when the generally understood and accepted basis of Israel's life would be changed. The two central themes of this vision were, first, that membership in the covenant community would be based upon circumcision of the heart and reception of the Spirit (Acts 2:16-18, quoting Joel; note also Deut. 30:6) and, second, that a widespread and general influx of Gentiles would occur (Acts 15:15-18, quoting Amos, Jeremiah, and Isaiah). On just what basis salvation would be extended to the Gentiles is not always clearly spelled out in the Old Testament, though it is assumed that they would enter into the salvation of the one God as Gentiles, not as proselytes (Acts 15:1-35).

Thus it was that John the Baptist invited people to "register" for membership in the imminent kingdom. The baptized remnant were to be on the lookout for the one who was to come, and they were to bring their ethical conduct into line with the life of the future messianic age. John declared unequivocally that he was merely a forerunner of the kingdom, announcing its arrival. He was not himself the messianic agent equipped to usher in the messianic day and to confer its blessings. "After me comes he who is mightier than I. . . . I have baptized you with water; but he will baptize you with the Holy Spirit" (Mk. 1:7-8).

John didn't offer a very detailed description of what the coming kingdom was going to be like. Yet he invited those looking forward to life in the messianic age to abandon the form of life of the old era, the form of life that was incurring the divine wrath. In their crossing over they were to adopt already the righteous ethical standards of the life of the age to come, bringing forth fruit befitting their repentance. "He who has two coats, let him share with him who has none; and he who has food, let him do likewise" (Lk. 3:11). It is significant that John, like Jesus later, received tax collectors and soldiers, prescribing for them the ethical reform demanded by the coming kingdom. Those who sought to survive the coming judgment and to enter into the new age of God's kingdom would need to repent, to turn around, and to line up with the way God was moving in history. The way to escape the "wrath to come" was to cross over without delay. Those responding to John's baptism were in effect admitting, "Yes, Israel has gone the wrong way. We hereby turn around and identify ourselves with the remnant that hopes to survive the divine sifting and judgment in order to inherit the blessings of the new age of the kingdom."

The Baptism of Jesus

"Then," says Matthew (3:13), "Jesus came from Galilee to the Jordan to John, to be baptized by him." This incident has puzzled many Christian readers since the early ages of the church. If John's was a baptism of repentance, but Jesus was sinless, why did he seek to receive this baptism? The question is raised already in the apocryphal gospel according to the Hebrews. According to that account the mother and brothers of Jesus proposed to go to John, saying, "Let us go and be baptized by him." But Jesus replied, "In what have I sinned that I should go and be baptized by him? Unless, perhaps, what I have just said is a sin of ignorance."[9]

The question of why Jesus sought baptism ceases to remain problematic if we see the event in the light of the situation just sketched. If God's hour had struck, and God was calling for a believing remnant of Israel to march into the future kingdom and to constitute the new messianic community of this era, then one would expect Jesus, like Moses, to be the first to step forward into the waters to lead this believing remnant forth.

Moses had lived in privilege rather than bondage. He wasn't personally in need of liberation. But he chose to identify with his oppressed people, undergoing their suffering and danger through the Red Sea to freedom, to Sinai, and to covenant life under God.

John the Baptist's mission was patterned after the original exodus from Egypt. In that light the important consideration is *not* personal sins that one might seek to wash away in a cultic act like that of an isolated individual at the Ganges. John's baptism meant moving with God in his purposes for a people. Such identification with God's purposes *did* mean leaving behind an old epoch and an old social, political, economic, and religious order. If one had been identified with that order, then moving with God required repentance, turning around to go the other way. But even if one had *not* been identified with the old order, one would want to move with God. Indeed, a person prophetically critical of the old order would be expected to be one of the foremost in turning from the old age and its order to the new age and its order.

The question, then, is not why Jesus sought baptism. The question is rather why anyone would think he should have avoided it. The essential conditions for receiving baptism were identification with God's people and the faith-expectation of God's imminent deliverance. Thus Jesus was foremost among those accepting the message of John, given his identification with Israel and his concern for the destiny of his people. He desired to have realized in Israel's life, and to experience in his own, that coming reign of God John was announcing.

Having spoken his amen to John's message, Jesus now found himself called, in the very act of baptism itself, to be the messianic instrument of bringing to fulfillment what John had announced. Jesus received the call through the Spirit of God and the heavenly voice, "This is my beloved Son, with whom I am well pleased (Mt. 3:17)." As commentators have noted, this is the first instance in the history of biblical thought of combining the two basic Old Testament themes of kingship and suffering. The "beloved Son" (Ps. 2) is God's anointed King whom God will use to restore Israel and whom God will give the nations as his heritage. The one in whom God is well pleased (Is. 42:1) is the suffering servant who redeems Israel and brings forth justice to the nations. Note again the two messianic expectations identified here: a renewal of Israel and the extension of Yahwist (Jehovah) faith to the Gentile world.

According to the Gospel of John (it is not mentioned in the synoptic Gospels), Jesus also engaged in a baptizing ministry alongside of John the Baptist (Jn. 3:22, 23), very appropriately endorsing the Johannine message of the kingdom. But when Jesus heard that the Pharisees discovered he "was making and baptizing more disciples than John," Jesus apparently desisted, implying that John's mission had to run its course and was not to be eclipsed prematurely. John's message was of God, and it had to have its day.

After John's arrest and during Jesus' public ministry, the practice of baptism seems to have been discontinued. The Gospels nowhere tell us why, but the church later resumed baptism on Christ's authority given in the so-called Great Commission (Mt. 28:19-20). We must conclude that this interim marked the transition from John's "forerunner" baptism to Christ's "Spirit and fire" baptism, a transition brought about by Jesus' own mission.

Jesus' mission is compared to that of Moses—delivering or leading out a people and bringing them into a new spiritual and social order. At the transfiguration, with Jesus approaching his passion, Moses and Elijah "appeared in glory and spoke of his departure [or exodus], which he was to accomplish at Jerusalem" (Lk. 9:31). As Moses delivered his people and brought them into covenant through personal suffering, so Jesus would deliver his people and bring them into the life of the messianic era through personal suffering.

Jesus thus fittingly called his mission a baptism. "I have a baptism to be baptized with; and how I am constrained until it is accomplished!" (Lk. 12:50). And when James and John asked for chief positions in the coming kingdom, he asked, "Are you able to drink the cup that I drink, or to be baptized with the baptism with which I am baptized?" In these sayings (which apart from references to John the Baptist and the Great Commission are Jesus' only uses of the term "baptism") Jesus called his passion a baptism. And Jesus described his passion also as a repetition of the sign of Jonah

(Mt. 12:38-41). Jonah typified the deportation and potential drowning and death of Israel in the sea of nations. But the deportation led instead to Israel's miraculous preservation and to Israel's witness to the nations for the sake of their salvation. In his death and resurrection, Jesus likewise crossed over into a new epoch; in that act he led out and brought into existence a new people—which included the Gentiles and thus inaugurated their divinely intended salvation.

Baptism in the Apostolic Church

Jesus' death and resurrection—his baptism of blood, his crossing over, his exodus—precipitated the resumption of baptism. According to Matthew 28:19-20, the risen Christ commissioned the apostles to make disciples of all nations, baptizing them and teaching them to observe all things he had commanded. And so the practice of baptism was resumed at Pentecost. Peter proclaimed the momentous news, "This Jesus God raised up, and of that we all are witnesses. Being therefore exalted at the right hand of God, and having received from the Father the promise of the Holy Spirit, he has poured out this which you see and hear. . . . Let all the house of Israel therefore know assuredly that God has made him both Lord and Christ, this Jesus whom you crucified" (Acts 2:32-33, 36). Since the reign of God announced by John the Baptist was now inaugurated, the doors of the kingdom stood open for others who wished to enter. "Repent, and be baptized every one of you in the name of Jesus Christ for the forgiveness of your sins; and you shall receive the gift of the Holy Spirit." No longer as in John's baptism did candidates say merely, "I want to be part of the messianic order *to come.*" Now they said, "I want to be part of the messianic reign that *has begun,* to share its salvation and blessings."

The connection between John's baptism and Christian baptism after Pentecost is quite logical. John baptized those declaring their intention to be part of the coming kingdom. Now at Pentecost the messianic era was inaugurated. It was not needful for those who had received John's baptism, such as the disciples, to be rebaptized. They had already earlier crossed over proleptically to adopt the life of the kingdom; they now participated in the first outpouring of its blessings. But it was not too late for others to cross over, to get on board, to become part of the launched messianic era and its blessings, though for them undergoing baptism and receiving the Spirit did not need to be two distinct events separated by a span of time.

The fact that baptism in water and baptism with the Spirit came in two stages in the lives of the apostles did not make this the normative pattern for others. The two-stage pattern in the lives of the apostles was a consequence of their living through the transition from the old era to the new. For them baptism by faith in anticipation of the kingdom and the actual inheritance of post-Pentecost life embraced a period of several years. After Pentecost this hiatus was closed, and the normal pattern of baptism became one act of believing in Christ and receiving his Spirit.

In the first period of the Christian movement baptism continued to be the sign by which believing Jews identified themselves with the kingdom movement. And for some time the first apostles spoke "the word to none except Jews" (Acts 11:19). Baptism meant crossing over into the new era God had ushered in, into the new Israel. It meant accepting the blessings and responsibilities of life in the messianic community, confessing Jesus as Christ and Lord.

Since one of the characteristics of the new messianic era was to be the accession of Gentiles to the faith, there soon was an influx of Gentile believers into the community of faith. The Great Commission commanded "making disciples of *all nations*, baptizing them...." The report of the Jerusalem conference in Acts 15 makes clear that even conservative Christian Jews conceded that the Old Testament itself anticipated that in the messianic day Gentiles would come to faith in the God of Israel and share in his salvation *as Gentiles.* In other words, Israel expected its faith to become worldwide in the messianic era. And since the first Jewish Christians claimed that the messianic era had arrived, they logically welcomed believing Gentiles into the messianic community. The sign by which Gentiles confessed their faith and were admitted to the community was the same as that of Christian Jews—baptism.

From the beginning baptism seems to have been considered the regularly accepted, unquestioned rite of entrance into the messianic community. In Acts "it is very clear that baptism is the normal, indeed the invariable, gateway to membership in the church."[10] With few exceptions baptism has continued in the Christian church to the present day, at least in theory and intention, as the definitive sign of entrance into the Christian way.

The New Testament Data

For those interested in the biblical data, perhaps for further personal or group study, I suggest a look at all the significant New Testament references to distinctively Christian baptism to find how it is there defined and practiced, taking into account only the direct and explicit statements that employ the term itself.

In the so-called Great Commission (Mt. 28:19-20), baptism is described as a command of the risen Lord. Baptism is to mark discipleship, it is to be administered in the triune name, and it is to be followed up by teaching in the way of Christ.

In Peter's Pentecost sermon (Acts 2:38-42) baptism signifies repentance and reception of the word of the gospel, it offers forgiveness of sins and the gift of the Spirit, and it calls for separation from "this crooked generation." Luke describes the consequences of baptism: those who were baptized were "added" to the church, and they devoted themselves to the apostolic teaching, fellowship, and worship.

In Philip's mission to the Samaritans (Acts 8:12-17), baptism followed "believing" the good news "about the kingdom of God and the name of Jesus Christ," or receiving the word (v. 14), and it is followed by the gift of the Spirit.

In Philip's baptism of the Ethiopian (Acts 8:37), baptism betokens believing in Christ as the Son of God (though we should note that the best ancient manuscripts do not have verse 37 of the King James Version).

In the conversion of Saul-Paul (Acts 9:18), we are told merely that Paul was baptized, though a preceding verse reports that he should be filled with the Spirit (v. 17). Obviously Paul's baptism also implied a coming to belief in Jesus as the Christ (v. 22) and Son of God (v. 20). In Paul's own account of his conversion before the Jerusalem crowd (Acts 22:1-21), he says that Ananias summoned him to "rise and be baptized, and wash away your sins, calling on his name" (the name of Jesus, no doubt). In his defense before Agrippa, however, Paul makes no mention of his baptism (Acts 26).

Acts 10:44-48 reports the baptism "in the name of Jesus Christ" of all who heard the word in Cornelius' house and who received the Holy Spirit just as the apostles received the Spirit at Pentecost.

Lydia was baptized, with her household, when "the Lord opened her heart to give heed to what was said by Paul" (Acts 16:14-15).

The Philippian jailer was baptized "with all his family" when he "believed" (in the Lord Jesus, one presumes), as a result of which he "rejoiced with all his household" (Acts 16:31-34).

According to Acts 18:8, Crispus, ruler of the synagogue in Corinth, "believed in the Lord, together with all his household." Indeed, "many of the Corinthians hearing Paul believed and were baptized."

Acts 19:1-5 reports the rebaptism in the name of the Lord Jesus of twelve John-the-Baptist disciples who had not received the Holy Spirit at their initiation into the Baptist movement. But the Spirit "came on them" at their baptism "when Paul had laid his hands upon them."

So much for Acts. In the epistles of the New Testament baptism is "into Christ," specifically "into his death," and is expected to issue in "newness of life," a life that is "freed from sin" (Rom. 6:4, 7. See also Col. 2:12).

Baptism is *not* into the name of Paul, according to 1 Corinthians 1:13. One infers that it is, instead, into the name of Christ. Baptism is "by one Spirit" and "into one body" (1 Cor. 12:13). The latter expression I take to mean the church.

According to Galatians 3:27 baptism is "into Christ"; it implies putting on Christ. Ephesians 4:5 speaks of one baptism and seems to imply that this baptism calls people into one hope, under one Lord, possessing one faith.

Finally, 1 Peter 3:21 designates baptism a salvation, "not as a removal of dirt from the body but as an appeal to God for a clear conscience, through the resurrection of Jesus Christ."

These are all the significant references to Christian baptism in the New Testament. Readers are invited to check them for themselves, using the pertinent excerpted sections from a Greek-English concordance reproduced below.° This list includes some references not listed above that do not contribute significantly to an understanding of the meaning of baptism. For example, 1 Corinthians 15 refers to baptism for the dead, which is incidental to another point Paul is making about resurrection. Hebrews 6:2 deplores a rehash of elementary doctrines concerning baptism and other things, a reference incidental to the writer's encouragement to his readers to go on to maturity.

It may be claimed with good reason that several other texts denote baptism and thus bear upon our subject, even if they do not use the term. Titus 3:5 speaks of the washing of regeneration (see also John 3:3, 5). Ephesians 5:26 speaks of the cleansing of the church "by the washing of water with the word." These texts may very possibly signify the rite of baptism, but they could also be figurative, so we are limiting ourselves to the texts containing an explicit mention of the term.

°Concordance material:[11]

βαπτίζω, baptizo.

Mat. 3:6. *were baptized* of him in Jordan,
11. I indeed *baptize* you with water
— he *shall baptize* you with the
13. unto John, *to be baptized* of him.
14. I have need *to be baptized* of thee,
16. Jesus, *when* he *was baptized,*
20:22. *to be baptized* with the baptism that I *am baptized* with?
23. and *be baptized* with the baptism that I *am baptized* with:
28:19. *baptizing* them in the name

Mar. 1:4. John did *baptize* in the wilderness,
5. *were* all *baptized* of him in the
8. I indeed *have baptized* you with water: but

he *shall baptize* you with the
9. *was baptized* of John in Jordan.
6:14. That John the *Baptist* was risen
7:4. except they *wash,* they eat not.
10:38. and *be baptized* with the baptism that I *am baptized* with?
39. and with the baptism that I *am baptized*
withal *shall* ye *be baptized:*
16:16. He that believeth and is *baptized* shall

Lu. 3:7. came forth *to be baptized* of him,
12. I indeed *baptize* you with water;
— he *shall baptize* you with the
21. when all the people were *baptized,* it

came to pass, that Jesus also *being baptized,*

7:29. *being baptized* with the baptism

30. themselves, *being* not *baptized* of him.

11:38. *had* not first *washed* before dinner.

12:50. I have a baptism *to be baptized* with;

Joh. 1:25. said unto him, Why *baptizest* thou then,

26. saying, I *baptize* with water:

28. Jordan, where John was *baptising.*

31. therefore am I come *baptizing* with

33. sent me *to baptize* with water,

— *which baptizeth* with the Holy Ghost.

3:22. there he tarried with them, and *baptized.*

23. John also was *baptizing* in Enon

— they came, and *were baptized.*

26. behold, the same *baptizeth,* and all

4:1. that Jesus made and *baptized* more disciples

2. Though Jesus himself *baptized* not,

10:40. place where John at first *baptized;*

Acts 1:5. John truly *baptized* with water;

— ye *shall be baptized* with the Holy Ghost

2:38. Repent, and *be baptized* every one of you

41. received his word *were baptized:*

8:12. *were baptized,* both men and women.

13. *when* he *was baptized,* he continued

16. only they were *baptized* in the name

36. what doth hinder me *to be baptized?*

38. Philip and the eunuch; and he *baptized* him.

9:18. forthwith, and arose, and *was baptized.*

10:47. that these should not *be baptized,*

48. commanded them *to be baptized*

11:16. John indeed *baptized* with water;

— ye *shall be baptized* with the Holy Ghost.

16:15. when she *was baptized,* and her

33. *was baptized,* he and all his,

18:8. hearing believed, and *were baptized.*

19:3. Unto what then *were* ye *baptized?*

4. John verily *baptized* with the

5. they *were baptized* in the name

22:16. arise, and *be baptized,* and wash away

Ro. 6:3. so many of us as *were baptized* into Jesus

Christ *were baptized* into his death?

1 Co. 1:13. *were* ye *baptized* in the name

14. that I *baptized* none of you,

15. that I *had baptized* in mine own name.

16. I *baptized* also the household of Stephanas besides, I know not whether I *baptized* any other.

17. Christ sent me not *to baptize,*

10:2. were all *baptized* unto Moses

12:13. by one Spirit *are* we all *baptized*

15:29. which are *baptized* for the dead,

— why *are* they then *baptized* for

Gal. 3:27. *have been baptized* into Christ

βαπτισμα, baptisma.

Mat. 3:7. Pharisees and Sadducees come to his *baptism,*

20:22. the *baptism* that I am baptized with?

23. with the *baptism* that I am

21:25. The *baptism* of John, whence was it?

Mar. 1:4. preach the *baptism* of repentance

10:38. the *baptism* that I am baptized with?

39. with the *baptism* that I am

11:30. The *baptism* of John, was (it) from

Lu. 3:3. preaching the *baptism* of repentance

7:29. baptized with the *baptism* of John.

12:50. I have a *baptism* to be baptized

20:4. The *baptism* of John, was it from

Acts 1:22. Beginning from the *baptism* of John,

10:37. the *baptism* which John preached;

13:24. the *baptism* of repentance to all

18:25. knowing only the *baptism* of John.

19:3. they said, Unto John's *baptism.*

4. with the *baptism* of repentance,

Ro. 6:4. with him by *baptism* into death,

Eph. 4:5. One Lord, one faith, one *baptism,*

Col. 2:12. Buried with him in *baptism,*

1 Pet. 3:21. (even) *baptism,* doth also now save us

βαπτισμός, baptismos.

Mat. 7:4. (as) the *washing* of cups, and pots,

Mar. 7:8. (as) the *washing* of pots and cups:

Heb. 6:2. Of the doctrine of *baptisms*, and of
    9:10. meats and drinks, and divers
        washings,

βαπτιστής, baptistees.

Mat. 3:1. In those days came John the *Baptist*,
    11:11. a greater than John the *Baptist*:
        12. from the days of John the *Baptist*
    14:2. This is John the *Baptist*;
        8. Give me here John *Baptist's* head
    16:14. (that thou art) John the *Baptist*:
    17:13. spake unto them of John the *Baptist*.

Mar. 6:24. The head of John the *Baptist*.
        25. the head of John the *Baptist*.
    8:28. they answered, John the *Baptist*:

Lu. 7:20. John the *Baptist* hath sent us
        28. a greater prophet than John the
            Baptist:
        33. John the *Baptist* came neither
    9:19. answering said, John the *Baptist*;

βύπτω, bapto.

Lu. 16:24. that he *may dip* the tip of his finger

Joh. 13:26. shall give a sop *when I have dipped*
        (it).

Rev. 19:13. clothed with a vesture *dipped* in
        blood:

Chapter 2

THE NEW TESTAMENT PATTERN

The Meaning of Baptism

Throughout Christian history baptism has always been connected in some sense with salvation. But is baptism necessary to salvation? If so, *how* does it save?

"In all parts of the New Testament," says one writer, "baptism is presupposed as normative for the acceptance of the Christian faith and entrance into the church. . . . The significance attributed to baptism by the apostolic writers shows that they viewed it as a means of grace."[12] The question of the necessity of baptism "would have sounded as strange to a first-generation Christian," continues this scholar, as the question of whether it is necessary to pray, to worship, to preach, or to accept the authority of Scripture.

If, as we have said in the previous chapter, baptism reflects Israel's experience in crossing the Red Sea and the Jordan, then baptism is as essential to salvation as the crossing of the Red Sea and Jordan were to Israel's deliverance from bondage in Egypt and realization of covenant life in the Promised Land. There is no possibility of participating in the salvation of the messianic community unless one crosses

41

over into its life! Since the apostolic church claimed that the mission of Jesus had inaugurated the messianic community, baptism was established as the condition of entrance into it.

It wasn't long in the history of baptism, however, before problems arose about the efficacy and meaning of baptism. If Israel's geographical crossing of the Red Sea and Jordan did not guarantee a new life for all Israelites or for all time, then baptism, which is not even a geographical move, is still more in danger of becoming a perfunctory rite, even if it is intended to mark a real transition into a new and spiritual life.

Baptism poses the danger of self-deception. Since baptism under normative conditions marks entrance upon the life of faith, people can cherish false assurances, presuming that the rite of baptism always perforce leads to faith. But it did not in the past and does not today always and inevitably lead to faith. It is possible to have instances of the rite that do not mark entrance upon the Christian way.

Does Baptism Save?

There are three possible answers to the problem of inauthentic instances of baptism. The *first* is the answer of sacramentalism—the insistence that baptism must in fact unfailingly effect what it is supposed to signify. This has been traditionally the position of the Catholic, Anglican, and Lutheran churches.

The *second* answer, usually a reaction to the first, is loss of confidence in or even abandonment of the sign. If there is a temptation to place unwarranted confidence in the rite of baptism itself, then the answer to the problem is to depreciate or eliminate the rite on which people are placing undue confidence, in order that their attention might be turned to the reality—spiritual life—that baptism is intended to signify. This is the position of the Salvation Army and of many Quakers.

In short, if it is possible (as experience and the observation of church history show) to apply water where there is no entrance upon salvation or to have salvation where no water was applied, there is a strong temptation to question the connection between the sign and the reality and to depreciate the rite out of concern for the reality.

It is worth observing that we cannot do without signs. Those groups that have discontinued baptism as the sign of Christian initiation must introduce some other generally understood and even regularized sign—for example, a pledge, or appearance at a "mourner's bench," or signing of a "decision card." They thus retain some recognized way of signifying faith, which shows that it is not a question of *whether* we will have a sign of entrance upon the way of faith but *what* sign we will use. Should we stay with the sign given us by the New Testament? Or may we switch to other signs?

We have convincing reasons to stay with the sign given us in the New Testament, even after two thousand years. Baptism calls the church back to, and keeps it grounded in, its foundation in Christ. We retain baptism for the same reason that we retain bread and the fruit of the vine in the Lord's supper rather than switching to potato chips and cola. The meaning of the Lord's supper is defined by what Christ said and did with his disciples, not by the welter of values revolving around potato chips and cola in modern civilization. So also incorporation into the church is defined by the events of salvation history given in the Bible—exodus and Jesus of Nazareth. To abandon the biblical pattern of initiation is to risk the loss of the biblical norm and quality of church life. Without question the health and well-being of the church are furthered by faithful continuation of the sign given us in the foundation of the church.

We should continue baptism also because it has the reflexive effect of reinforcing the grace and strengthening the faith it recognizes. Where the Holy Spirit creates faith, there the church's recognition of such faith has the "feedback" effect of clarifying faith, leading the baptized person into congregational involvement, supplying assurance, nurture, and growth. In the absence of baptism, faith can be impoverished, and in extreme cases faith may even perish.

Baptism incorporates the element of confirmation by lifting the act of faith out of individual isolation and giving it community support. In the early church of the third and fourth centuries, confirmation was an integral part of the complete baptismal liturgy. It took place immediately after the baptism in water. Confirmation represented the church's "amen" to God's saving action upon an individual. Hence baptism performs the function of reinforcing faith.

We can see the same principle in the analogous institution of ordination to the Christian ministry. The mere act of laying hands on persons does not of itself make ministers. They must have a spiritual gift and a call. But where God is giving the call, there ordination strengthens the gift, sets it free, and provides the church's confirmation of the call.

Or take the illustration of marriage. A ceremony does not by itself make a marriage. There must be love there. But if love is present it is expressed and enhanced by the ceremony. Many a relationship has been preserved by this formal act of crossing over into the estate of marriage, this commitment, this explicit personal and public recognition in a wedding ritual of the reality of love. So we can't play off the ceremony and love against each other as some do, saying that they don't want a formal institutional thing like marriage to get in the way of a "beautiful relationship." The reality without the ritual may be there. We call it common law marriage. But much is lost in the absence of the sign.

There is a *third* answer, finally, to the question of the saving efficacy of baptism, and that is to understand and preserve the integrity of the Christian way and then to rightly use baptism as the effectual sign of entrance upon this Christian way, neither insisting on automatic sacramentalist efficacy nor depreciating the rite of baptism. What is the reality New Testament baptism intends to signify?

The Meaning of Baptism

One way of trying to define what baptism should mean is to summarize the New Testament texts on it. Using this approach, the World Council of Churches Commission on Faith and Order says:

> Baptism is the sign of new life through Jesus Christ. It unites the one baptized with Christ and with his people. Baptism is participation in Christ's death and resurrection (Rom. 6:3-5; Col. 2:12); a washing away of sin (1 Cor. 6:11); a new birth (Jn. 3:5); an enlightment by Christ (Eph. 5:14); a reclothing in Christ (Gal. 3:27); a renewal by the Spirit (Tit. 3:5); the experience of salvation from the flood (1 Pet. 3:20-21); an exodus from bondage (1 Cor. 10:1-2); and a liberation into a new humanity in which barriers of division whether of sex or race or social status are transcended (Gal. 3:27-28; 1 Cor. 12:13).

The images are many but the reality is one.

Another way of trying to preserve the meaning of baptism is to identify its essential features. Using a key text, Acts 2:38-42, we can note four basic features. Baptism as entrance upon the Christian way signifies (1) acknowledgment of Jesus as Messiah, (2) reception of the Holy Spirit, (3) incorporation into the messianic community, and (4) moral transformation or renewal, forgiveness of sins. Let us elaborate upon each of these briefly.

into Jesus as Lord

1. In the New Testament Christian baptism is inescapably connected with the name of *Jesus.* Baptism is into Christ or into his name. Baptism signifies believing that Jesus is the Messiah, and it implies a commitment to act accordingly— to take up the life of the messianic age. To confess Jesus as the Christ is not only a claim about a historic fact. It is a readiness to live the kind of life inaugurated by that event.

Baptism thus signifies *eschatological life.* To believe in Christ means to cross over into the messianic era as part of the recreated community and to adopt the righteous life of the age to come, tasting its joys and blessings, but also incurring persecution from the people of this present evil age. Baptism generates a hope for the fulfillment of God's purposes in a second advent, purposes put in process by the first advent. And to die and rise with Christ in baptism carries the promise of future life in and with him.

Baptism thus signifies discipleship of Christ. To be baptized is to take up the way of Jesus, to be united with him, to demonstrate in one's life the nature or mind of Christ. In Paul's phrase, baptism begins life "in Christ." In short, baptism is completely Jesus Christ oriented.

receiving Holy Spirit

2. In the New Testament baptism implies simultaneously receiving life from God's *Holy Spirit.* To be baptized is to receive the Spirit of the new age promised by the prophets and by Jesus. It is to be empowered with the life of the Spirit, to be given his companionship. To be baptized and to receive the Spirit means to be gifted by the Spirit (symbolized by laying on of hands) and ordained to a correspondingly appropriate calling or task. The baptized life is nothing less than divine life itself coming to dwell within us.

3. <u>Baptism implies membership in the *redeemed community*</u>. Baptism achieves reconciliation, in which the alienations and estrangements of the old age are overcome. Separation from the world leads to participation (koinonia) in the church. Through membership in the church people cease to live in lonely isolation. "We are called to recognize that a purely private relationship to Christ cannot exist, nor a bestowal of the Spirit given to be enjoyed on our own, as it were, in isolation from the Christian fellowship. Koinonia is a key term of the Christian life, connoting fellowship in the Holy Spirit with Christ and with his saints, and it takes its rise in baptism to Christ and the Body."[13]

The believer is baptized by the church, not self-baptized. To begin with, he receives the invitation of the gospel from someone who is already a member of the body of Christ. And then it is the church that hears and recognizes the authenticity of the confession of faith. And finally baptism according to biblical thought entails binding oneself to the regenerate assembly.

The membership established by baptism is simultaneously local and universal, not just one of these. Baptism is into the church of Christ, not merely into the church at, say, Philippi. If it were only baptism into the local church, such would be valid only locally, and transfer to Ephesus would require a new baptism. Being universally valid, baptism according to the New Testament model is valid also for any or every local assembly.

But the membership in the universal church of Christ does not render local membership unnecessary or even optional. Instead it makes local membership mandatory, because the New Testament knows of no church except one that finds actual embodiment at Antioch, Corinth, Rome, or some other specific place.

commitment
to living
a new
way of
life.

4. Baptism in the New Testament means *a new ethical life*. This is already implied in each of the foregoing and should not need separate mention, but because the point is frequently overlooked today in contrast with apostolic times, it bears separate emphasis. Baptism means death to an old way of life and resurrection with Christ into a new way. Called regeneration, this entrance upon a new life involves acceptance of a new master; it is symbolized as putting off old garments and putting on new ones (which, it seems, was practiced literally in the patristic era, when baptism involved stripping naked for the baptismal "bath").

This new ethical life is not something formal and external, something postured—a moral resolution or the turning of a new leaf. It is more than the absence of specified sinful acts. It is the realization of a new nature.

As noted earlier, Jewish proselyte baptism was accompanied by careful teaching on the meaning of conversion from the old life to the new. So also biblical scholars discern in the New Testament—in the pages of the epistles especially—the outlines of an apostolic instruction that accompanied baptism. Here is one example, conflated from several New Testament texts.

> You received from us how you ought to walk in ... holiness, to abstain from fornication, fleshly desires, in sanctification (of the Spirit), not in passionate desires, in ignorance or cupidity, for you are not called in uncleanness (unholiness), but holiness (by) His (holy) Spirit. Concerning love of brethren ... love one another, doing your own business, not interfering, with concern for those without (so as to glorify God), not returning evil for evil, but seeking good.[14]

Such texts, which run like refrains through the New Testament, show that the primitive church took meticulous care to spell out the ethical dimensions of taking up the Christian walk. Baptismal candidates were not left in ignorance about what their act implied. Such teaching, of course, consisted not merely of verbal instruction. The church was a model of the life of the kingdom. In life and word it presented the whole gospel, making sure the nature of Christian life was not shortchanged. Thus converts came to clarity on the meaning of their step of faith.

Misunderstandings of Baptism

At various times and places people in the church have unfortunately considered these implications of baptism as separable and even optional. For example, it has been widely held that baptism might convey forgiveness but not necessarily a new nature; or that it might confer spiritual life but not require church membership; or that it might offer forgiveness of sin but not the gift of the Spirit; or that it might involve church membership but not regeneration.

In a proper understanding and practice of baptism, all these elements must be held together in a balanced and holistic unity. Because some of these distortions are fairly common, let us examine them briefly.

1. Baptism is sometimes seen as forgiveness without ethical renewal. In too much of Western church history baptism has meant almost exclusively the washing away of original sin or remission of past sins. On this view baptism is considered absolution, a cancellation of charges or remission of punishment, merely a new formal status before the moral-legal authority of God. But the New Testament shows that to be *forgiven* is to be *given*—to be given a new heart and attitude, the Spirit of Christ. Paul insists that baptism leads to a newness of life in which the believer is no longer "enslaved to sin."

2. Baptism may be viewed as new life in Christ but without the requirement of church membership. For some reason it has become fairly common in some free church circles to baptize people into Christ's universal church without requiring any concrete commitment to a local fellowship. This violates basic New Testament teaching.[15] How is it possible to become a child of God and not accept the consequent responsibilities of life in the family of God? Or to be indwelt by the Holy Spirit and not share (koinonia) in the community of faith.

It must be admitted that the churches have, to some extent, brought this upon themselves. Churches have too often misdefined membership to carry extraneous meanings not essential to the life of the kingdom, and some Christians then have protested and sought to avoid these extraneous meanings of church membership. But one mistake does not correct another. Membership must first be biblically defined and then made normative.

What should church membership actually involve? Here the most common issues immediately crowd in upon us, questions about attendance requirements, financial obligations, and the like. The crucial thing about such issues is *how* we go about answering them rather than how detailed we make the specific definitions or prescriptions of membership. The temptation beckons us to define membership by multiplying the requirements about attendance, residence, financial support, or conformity to the cultural mores of the congregation. But it is better, I think, to define membership in terms of the marks given in the New Testament. Such is not an escape into generalities, but establishes the needed frame of reference for a more detailed discussion of the requirements and duties of church membership.

In a discussion of responsibility in marriage, we should

not begin with disputes about who does the dishes on Tuesday nights, for even if we do, we must soon move to a broader understanding and acceptance of the meaning of marriage as a whole. In a similar way covenant must be grasped as the essence of life in Christ; covenant is the basis of functioning membership standards, standards which must be spelled out clearly.

3. Baptism may be considered a forgiveness in Christ that does not yet include the "baptism" of the Holy Spirit. One of the tragedies (the word is not too strong) of traditional Protestant Christianity in both charismatic and mainline churches is the common notion that Christian life is possible without the Holy Spirit, and that the infilling or baptism of the Spirit is a second work of grace, or at least a separate and distinct experience in the course of the Christian life. For charismatics or Pentecostals this experience is, of course, most desirable, even urgent. For staid church people it is strictly optional, perhaps even undesirable. But both agree baptism with the Spirit is separable from initial salvation and baptism in water.

[handwritten margin note: wrong to separate baptism in the Spirit from conversion & water baptism]

Here, as in many other aspects of religious life, experience tends to follow the way people are led to think. They are taught in the first place to see baptism as mere absolution, mere "forgiveness" without power, joy, freedom, and peace. And then they are led to expect an effervescent or ecstatic experience of the Spirit that derives a good deal of its character from being divorced from the initial Christian experience of forgiveness, faith in Christ, membership in the church, and ethical life. Naturally both are distorted—forgiveness and the baptism of the Spirit—whenever one of them is divorced from the other and sought and accepted for itself alone. The remedy for such distorted notions of initial faith and subsequent baptism of the Spirit is for the church to keep the components in proper connection. They will then receive a correct definition and expression.

What about the claim, though, that the baptism of the Spirit is a second and separate event? I personally think there are several explanations possible for this claim. First, in some cases the so-called baptism of the Spirit represents the real, initial conversion of the individual in question, and an earlier alleged Christian experience was not yet authentic Christian life. Second, in some cases the so-called baptism of the Spirit is an effervescent experience people have been persuaded to seek which doesn't add anything significant to their Christian life. Third, in most cases Christians have been cheated out of a full and normative experience of grace precisely because these stereotyped options have been the only ones available to them: the idea of conversion as simplistic "forgiveness of sins" and then the idea of the Spirit as simplistic ecstasy. Consequently, it takes a long time before many believers finally inherit that complete life of love, joy, freedom, peace, righteousness, hope, and power that is intended to be every Christian's baptismal birthright.

4. Perhaps most common today, especially among Mennonites, is the notion that baptism implies little more than church membership. Church membership may, of course, be held to have some consequence for a person's ultimate destiny, but in practice baptism signifies basically social conformity, a readiness to "settle down" and to recognize the social and cultural values of church membership. In too many cases not much sense of spiritual renewal surrounds the rite, little sense of "crossing over."

In the New Testament baptism does, of course, include membership in the church. But this membership presupposes a spiritual transaction—a call, a new birth, a divine act of ingrafting that goes far beyond conventional socialization.

Meanwhile, what about baptism under the inadequate or shortchanged conceptions just discussed? Are those people "saved" who claim forgiveness without church membership? Obviously one cannot make a blanket judgment on a wide range of actual cases. But let us use the illustration of marriage. Suppose two people have been properly married in church, have achieved a satisfactory support arrangement, and have even reached a satisfactory sexual relationship—on those occasions when they visit each other; but apart from occasional visits, they do not live together to share the task of conjointly rearing their children. Are they married? I can imagine many people saying, "That's no marriage!" And yet, if pressed, we would concede that technically they are married. Nevertheless, we would instinctively see some misunderstanding of marriage here, whatever its origin, and we would urge removal of this misunderstanding so that such people could bring their lives into line with the full meaning and blessings of marriage.

So it is with baptism. If New Testament believers were to return to our world and observe baptisms taking place without church membership, they would likely exclaim, "That's no baptism!" Our churches must teach the full-orbed biblical meaning of baptism to bring people in baptism to their rightful spiritual heritage.

To avoid distortions in the church's thought and practice of baptism and to preserve a healthy church, we must keep all of the New Testament's teaching about baptism before us and conform our practice to it. The various elements of baptism just discussed are not, according to the New Testament, separable components among which one might pick and choose. They are related and mutually inclusive, mutually implicated, a glorious whole. We are not at liberty, for example, to make baptism mean forgiveness but not Holy

Spirit infusion, or Holy Spirit infusion but not a change of ethical life. We must remember to keep all of the elements together, else we end up with a short-changed definition and an impoverished practice. Perhaps in some cases we run the risk of practicing a rite so far removed from its New Testament norms as to be spurious.

Grace and Faith

Theology has tended to name grace and faith as the two essentials in the meaning of baptism, the two irreducible components. Baptism is supposed to signify the intersection of these two realities. Grace is God's action, faith the human response, and both are essential for a valid baptism. Grace and faith do not, however, stand in absolute symmetry in this formula, because grace is prior to faith and is the source of faith. The love and power of God reach into the lives of people and generate in them the response of faith, drawing such people into the life of the kingdom of God. Since spiritual life is a product of grace, baptism in the New Testament takes place only upon the condition of faith. Baptism thus identifies those who believe and becomes the expression of their coming to faith.

In the New Testament baptism is thus always considered the work of divine grace. Baptism represents the activity of God's Word and Spirit in creating spiritual life. And baptism is the church's overt recognition of this prior work of God, this act of prevenient grace. Faith is therefore nothing less than a corollary of grace, being the work of grace.

We are using the term faith here in its full biblical sense. It is more than believing something to be true, more even than just trusting in God in an existential, private, inner, individualistic sense. Faith encompasses transformation of heart and mind, a new style of life, a new pattern of human relationships—in short, life in the messianic community under the rule of God.

Since faith is a corollary of grace, grace must not be claimed as a theoretical truth, an abstraction that operates apart from faith, because grace can be appropriated only by faith. Conversely, faith is the actualization of grace. A phony or imagined faith, a faith generated out of one's own power, is of course not of grace, and thus not true faith. It is time therefore that some theologians who should know better cease disparaging believers baptism as a reversion to works. It is possible, of course, to have spurious faith. And if that problem arises, one must deal with it. But let us not pit faith against grace as if insistence upon faith in baptism were a threat to the recognition of grace.

To baptize where faith is not present is to violate the truth of grace, because it is to baptize where grace has not been realized. For baptism as a mark of faith is intended to be precisely this mark of realized grace—that is, actual faith in the baptized—not just the hope of faith some time in the future, not just the faith of the baptizer or sponsor or church. Baptism in the New Testament marks the appearance of faith in the one baptized. As one writer notes, "In every baptism which Luke records, belief, hearing, or repentance is expressly mentioned as the concomitant of the rite, and always prior in time."[16]

The foregoing has implied what has traditionally been called a sacrament. A sacrament has often been defined as "an outward and visible sign of an inward and spiritual grace." In itself baptism is a rite or ceremony involving ordinary water (H_2O). But the rite is intended to denote a spiritual reality. One can, of course, have the spiritual reality without the sign, as we have noted. It would be foolish to say there never have been believers who were not baptized, for there have no doubt been many such. There can be spiritual life even when no water has been applied, either because baptism was not possible or because the church was remiss in its responsibility. One can also have the sign without the spiritual reality it is supposed to signify; that is, one can apply water when there is no spiritual life. And the water ritual does not of itself produce such life.

Both situations are definitely to be deplored. The church should not apply water except where it discerns the appearance of spiritual life, and when it discerns the appearance of spiritual life it should not be remiss but respond with the application of water. In short, where faith appears, the church should baptize to signify its recognition of God's gift of faith. In that sense Christian baptism is intended to be a true and living sign or sacrament according to the classic definition of that term—"the sign and the thing signified." That is, the sign and the spiritual reality to which it points should be kept together.

Coincidence of Sign and Reality

The meaning of baptism given in the New Testament offers an answer to the two questions that constantly recur in the life of the church: whom to baptize, and when. Concerning the first, the question of whom to baptize, the apostolic church quite simply baptized those who believed in Christ, received the Spirit, joined the messianic community, and lived the righteous life of the new age. It baptized those in whom the grace of God awakened living faith. This answer likely raises in many people's minds, however, the question of whether it is possible to discern, as confidently as we seem to assume, the operation of grace and faith?[17]

In reply we must say that the New Testament idea of baptism implies not only that we *can* but that we *should* be able to discern where regeneration occurs. As one writer points out, the New Testament in several places indicates caution concerning a candidate.[18] "What is to prevent my being baptized?" (Acts 8:36). "Can any one forbid water for baptizing these people who have received the Holy Spirit *just as we have?*" (Acts 10:47). "Who was I that I could withstand God?" (Acts 11:17).

These texts show that candidates for baptism were not received indiscriminately. Rather the presumption went the other way. The church tended to *decline* to baptize unless some positive and convincing evidence presented itself to justify baptism, for there might be some obstacle to baptism. The church felt the need to test professions of faith, and the responsibility rested upon the convert (or a sponsor) to provide evidence of the authenticity of his or her conversion.

The New Testament furthermore implies that the church possesses the requisite criteria for discerning the work of the Spirit. Members of the body of Christ have been forgiven, have been united with Christ, have received the Spirit, and have been regenerated. Being thus gifted with spiritual life, they are able to recognize those instances about them where this experience is reduplicated in the lives of other converts. As Peter says concerning the household of Cornelius, "Can any one forbid water for baptizing these people who have received the Holy Spirit *just as we have?*" (Acts 10:47). And before the Jerusalem elders Peter says similarly, "The Holy Spirit fell on them *just as on us* at the beginning. . . . If then God gave the same gift to them *as he gave to us* . . . who was I that I could withstand God?" (Acts 11:15, 17; emphasis added). So even if the church begins with appropriate hesitation, it proceeds with confidence where the Spirit bears unambiguous witness to his own saving work.

Those churches who claim they are unable to discern

instances of regeneration nevertheless do proceed, and with considerable boldness, to carry on the practice of baptism; and even with them some discrimination of candidates takes place. For if the church will not baptize on the basis of the gift of the Spirit, it will do so on some other criterion, the most common being that of natural birth. According to the New Testament, the proper subjects of baptism are those whom God calls, forgives, unites with Christ, grants his Holy Spirit, those whom he regenerates, ethically renews, and incorporates into his church.

The related question is *when* to baptize. Because it is not always easy to keep sign and reality together, some Christian traditions apply the sign according to some other criterion than the appearance of faith. They then insist that the reality must be there whether it is or is not—(*ex opere operato*—objective grace, or baptismal regeneration, it may be called). Despite (or because of?) this use of baptism, many of the baptized never do come to experience new life in Christ and the Spirit. Or the church develops a second sacrament or sign to mark the actual appearance of faith—confirmation perhaps (though that too can become routine), or the signing of a decision card. Where living faith does make its appearance in the life of someone earlier baptized, churches often fail to recognize such regeneration in any official or formal way. They have no provision in their liturgy or church order for this purpose. All that is available or possible is for interested fellow Christians to rejoice informally in the newfound faith of someone who is ostensibly already a Christian.

Some Christian traditions take the opposite approach; instead of applying the sign without the reality, they want to make so sure of the reality that they do not apply the sign until long after spiritual life is evident. This postponement of baptism may be called probation. But here too baptism has ceased to be a living sign and has instead become merely a retrospective report. Where this pattern has become institutionalized, the church usually again creates a new sign to express the initial act of faith—raised hand, a trip to the altar, or a signed decision card—applying baptism only later as a formality, an afterthought. In revivalist circles this decision card becomes in effect a "baptism in ink." Such a new rite no doubt seeks to be ecumenical and therefore to avoid those divisive issues about baptism that have separated denominations. But it compounds the problem by not keeping baptism connected with the awakening of faith. For that matter it often removes conversion from the setting and involvement of the congregation.

According to the pattern of the New Testament, baptism should be administered when faith appears. Early church converts would not have distinguished their conversion and baptism as two separable events. In the words of one writer, "Baptism is more than a recognition of what has happened; it recognizes that something is happening."[19] That is, baptism should be administered when the new birth occurs, when persons in faith cross over, putting on the new life in Christ. On this question the pattern in the New Testament, so far as we can discern it, is consistent: baptism is administered at the beginning of new spiritual life and as its sign.

Baptism is administered at the time of conversion regardless of the number of candidates involved. The New Testament speaks of a single baptism (the Ethiopian), of groups (Lydia and company), or of a large mass of people (Pentecost). Thus God's work of grace may not necessarily call individuals only one at a time. There may be a number of persons baptized at once. On the other hand, we need not wait for an entire class of candidates. In this matter the timing should be observed regardless of the number of candidates for baptism.

There is no justification in the biblical pattern for collecting a class of catechumens for baptism at a certain season of the church year—Easter, for example—a pattern that developed in the church some years after the time of the apostles. The issue here is not whether or not to have instruction. As noted above, the church of the New Testament likely did offer baptismal instruction, but it did so alongside of the work of the Holy Spirit. For example, Acts 2:38-40 says that Peter spoke "many other words" at Pentecost in instructing the converts there about saving themselves "from this crooked generation."

The church must follow up baptism with the ministry of teaching. Much traditional church practice stresses teaching *before* baptism and in preparation for it. Too often this teaching ends at baptism. But if, as we hold, baptism marks the beginning of Christian life, then baptism marks the beginning also of discipleship-learning, to which there is no end short of death.

Believers baptism underscores the proper sequence of what biblical scholars distinguish as *kerygma* and *didache*. Kerygma is proclamation that doesn't assume faith in the hearer but summons the hearer to it. Didache is teaching that does assume faith. In between proclamation and teaching we recognize the church's word accompanying baptism itself—*catechesis*. Kerygma says, "Repent and believe the good news. Be baptized for the remission of your sins, and you shall receive the gift of the Holy Spirit." *Catechesis* says, "Do you believe that Jesus is the Christ? If so, be informed of all that this act means in putting off the old life and putting on Christ." *Didache* then says, "Since you have been

Do
enuf
instruction
to be sure
candidate
1) claims Jesus as Lord
2) Is putting on new life
B. Then baptize
c. Then continue
instruction after
baptism.

raised with Christ, seek the things that are above. Walk in love, be joyful in Spirit, serve one another...."

Proclamation and teaching communicate the same gospel, but there is a difference, a "before" and "after," a difference created by an event, an actual happening. This event is the creation of a covenant, a new status, a new relationship, a new life.

Seen in this light, teaching becomes an essential activity following baptism. Sometimes newly baptized converts falter (or the church hesitates to baptize some converts for fear of their faltering) not because the converts do not possess real spiritual life, but because the church treats baptism as a kind of termination of its special ministry to converts it fails to offer them the kind of post-baptismal encouragement, instruction, support, and nurture needed for Christian growth and for life and service in the church.

Is it possible to concentrate in one moment all that is signified in baptism? Widespread opinion has it that salvation is a process spread out over an extended period of time. Some people have sudden conversions, granted ("Paul Christians" they may be called); but others, perhaps the majority, develop gradually in faith ("Timothy Christians"). Isn't the death and resurrection with Christ an "I die daily," as Paul held? Is a datable conversion normative or even normal?

Let us clarify immediately that we must distinguish two things, the *beginning* of spiritual life and *growth* in it. To my knowledge no one questions the fact of development and growth *within* the Christian life, but can one locate its beginning? We must note that for better or worse the act of baptism is a datable event. To my knowledge no church in Christendom makes the application of water an extended process covering the span of growth in faith—a cumulative spray mist applied over an entire lifetime. The point is not facetious. There is likely good reason why the people of biblical times found baptism an apt sign. Process rituals were no doubt available to them. But they chose an event sign such as baptism because it was a fitting symbol for the reality it denoted.

According to the New Testament, baptism intends to mark an event. It denotes the repudiation of sin and the world in favor of life in the kingdom. It represents forgiveness of sin and separation from the world, death to the old life, crossing over into the life of the age to come. Though the New Testament does not dwell unnecessarily on the details of the old sinful life but focuses on the nature of the spiritual life, it is quite capable of realistically describing the sinful life. The sinful life is "immorality, impurity, passion, evil desire, and covetousness...." It is "anger, wrath, malice, slander ... foul talk" and lying (Col. 3:5-10). In contrast is the life to which the baptized person has turned: "compassion, kindness, lowliness, meekness, and patience," forbearance, forgiveness, love, peace, thankfulness, service, and joy (Col. 3:12-17).

Baptism itself represents the act of turning, of reorientation and reintegration. Baptism implies "crisis" in the original Greek sense of that word—that is, decision. As noted earlier, baptism carries over the theme of the exodus, when Israel left behind an old world with its evils and came under the protection and authority of the pillar of cloud and fire; this led on to Sinai, covenant, and—at least in intention—to life under the will of God in the Promised Land.

It will not suffice to plead that in New Testament times conversions were usually decisive because Christianity was a new faith but that today the situation is different. The event nature of conversion and baptism is rooted in the reality of life, sin, and grace. Sin and grace stand in polarity with each other, in tension; there cannot be an indefinite hesitation between them. The gospel is attuned to this situation. It precipitates decision, a reorientation, a crossing over. Where the message of the New Testament is faithfully presented, there people are summoned, brought to decision, and enabled to cross over into the life of the new age.

The New Testament Model

We have just reviewed what I would like to call the model or pattern of baptism in the New Testament. This pattern involves the adult convert crossing over into Christianity from Judaism or from the Greco-Roman Gentile world, symbolized by baptism upon confession of faith. While there are a few points in this model on which we could wish more theological clarity, and while we might have some way to go before we live up to what is already clear to us, our main problem is not understanding it but applying it. As one writer says, "On fundamental matters of the Christological, ecclesiological, eschatological, and ethical meaning of baptism, there has been widespread agreement among recent New Testament scholars, whatever their denominational allegiance."[20] Disagreement arises chiefly when we turn to the subject of how baptism applies to children of the church.

The New Testament model has demonstrated its power and appeal throughout history, not only in the church of the first few centuries, but also in modern history since the time of the Reformation and the church's recovery of the biblical imperatives of mission and evangelism. As long as there are non-Christian people in the world who respond to the gospel, the New Testament model will remain alive and valid.

Up to the present this model is accepted and practiced by

almost all churches, from Roman Catholic to Pentecostal ones. Wherever and whenever an unbaptized adult from the non-Christian world comes to Christian faith, it is the norm for such a person to be baptized and incorporated into the body of Christ in accord with the classic New Testament pattern.

We can state it almost as an axiom, then, that according to the New Testament, in the time after Pentecost baptism is the normative sign of coming to faith. Someone who becomes a believer should be baptized, and conversely someone who is baptized should be a believer. And since believing is the condition for membership in Christ's church, the church has quite properly made baptism the sign of entrance into the church. These understandings we will therefore accept as a basis for further discussion.

Despite all of the multitudinous problems that have surrounded the practice of baptism through the ages, several facts remain that should be kept in view. First, with very few exceptions, all churches have retained the practice of believers baptism, even if it takes a minority position alongside of infant baptism. That is, even pedobaptist churches baptize upon faith those converts who were *not* baptized in their infancy and who come from unbelief to faith after childhood. Second, almost all churches contend, at least in theory, that everyone who desires to be or to remain in the church, regardless of whether he or she was baptized in infancy or as an adult, should possess and show evidence of faith. We might question the adequacy of the definition of faith held by many churches in many times and places, but the practice of catechism and confirmation, the Catholic rule requiring annual participation in the mass—these and other considerations show that all branches of the church throughout its history have rather consistently attempted to connect faith and baptism. This at least has been the churches' vision, intention, and profession.

The presumption that baptism and faith are or should be correlative has been so strong, so fundamental in the Christian consciousness through the ages, that the onus has always rested upon those who have departed from the immediate and direct connection of personal faith and baptism in the New Testament model to justify their departure from that model. In essence, the question is whether the act of baptism should consistently be conjoined immediately and directly with coming to faith, or whether in some cases (usually in the case of children of believers) baptism can anticipate faith and spiritual life by a dozen or more years. It is to this problem we now turn.

Chapter 3

THE DISCIPLINE AND INSTRUCTION OF THE LORD
Children of the Church

The big question which arises repeatedly in the history of Christianity is whether the New Testament model of baptism fits the situation of children of the church who grow up nurtured in the faith. Isn't the situation of children of the church in some sense different from that of people who have been born and have grown up in the non-Christian world outside the church and who come to faith in adult life?

The long-standing and by now unquestioned position of the majority of people in Christendom is that the situation of children of believers is so significantly different that in their case baptism should be administered in infancy. To people imbued with the New Testament model of believers baptism, this position seems so much a deviation from the New Testament model that they can only consider the rise of infant baptism in the past and its continuation today a perversion of New Testament Christianity.

The Situation of Children of the Church Is Different
My years of study and reflection on this subject have

persuaded me that the situation of children of the church *is* different from that of persons in the non-Christian world. I think, however, that the recognition of this fact does not lead logically to infant baptism. Nevertheless, despite the confusion and inconsistency that has characterized the infant baptism tradition (some of which we will discuss later), this tradition has tried to make an important point that Christians of the believers baptism tradition have not been willing to hear. Let us look briefly at the argument that the situation of children of the church is different from that of people in the non-Christian world. (I prefer to speak of "children of the church" for reasons that will become clear in the rest of this book. Incidentally, by children of the church I mean not just little tots but all those from infancy to adolescence whom the church can bring under its ministry and care, and that includes not only children of church members.)

The special situation of children of the church is illustrated already by the exodus, which we identified earlier as the archetype of baptism. After Israel's deliverance from bondage in Egypt and entrance as a covenant community into the Promised Land, their descendants did not need to return to bitter Egyptian bondage in each generation in order to make their own difficult crossing through the Red Sea and the Jordan. Subsequent generations had the privilege of growing up under the blessings of covenant life in the land.

The difference is not accidental. The situation of subsequent generations was *intended* to be different. It was not God's will that each generation grow up in bondage. The purpose of the original deliverance under Moses was to create a new kind of human society where people could grow up in a redeemed community, the kind of community God intended already in the creation.

To grow up in the Promised Land did not imply the right to forget Egypt. Each generation was supposed to remember, the purpose of the deliverance—to be a genuinely new kind of human community. Each generation was supposed to appropriate for itself and to keep covenant faith.

To this end Joshua instructed representatives of the twelve tribes who crossed the Jordan to erect a stone cairn in the Jordan as a memorial to their descendants so that they would remember that their forebears had crossed that way. Generations to follow were to remind themselves from this cairn of the need to live out the significance of the first generation's redemption from Egypt, their baptism in the Red Sea and the Jordan. And when Israel later forgot what kind of people it was supposed to be as a consequence of its having crossed over from Egypt into the land, God took them back to the wilderness in the exile for a renewed crossing.

Israel's experience sets an example for the Christian community. One of the consequences of the salvation of non-Christian people today—indeed, one of its purposes—is to establish a new environment for their children, so that these children do not need to grow up in a non-Christian setting but can be brought up in the discipline and instruction of the Lord.

The situation of children of the covenant community is different, then, from that of first-generation adult converts. The difference does not lie, of course, in any special gene structure, for children of believers are born with the usual human nature. Children born and reared within the Christian community are, however, shaped by the instruction and example of the life of the people of God. They are nurtured in biblical history and doctrine and thus are beneficiaries of the blessings of the Christian way. Children reared in Christian homes and churches are also sheltered from undesirable worldly influences to the extent that this is possible.

Yes, the situation of children of the community of faith is different from that of the sinful world. *According to God's purposes it is intended to be different.* The grace of God is, of course, big enough to rescue the worst of sinners, as the apostle Paul exulted. Yet thankful as we are for that fact, we are thankful for a still more ultimate grace of God—namely, that it is possible to save people from entering upon a sinful life in the first place. The cycle of sinful lives need not be repeated. Once saved, sinners can and should by the grace of God nurture their children (and, indeed, any and all children they can reach and influence) in the life of the kingdom so that these children may appropriate the life of faith for themselves when they reach the age of discretion.

The Other Biblical Model

We can claim, then, that alongside of the impressive and conspicuous pattern of dramatic crisis conversion and baptism that dominates the New Testament, the Scriptures offer a second pattern, less sensational and yet representing a higher ideal. It is the pattern of nurture in Christian principles from childhood, nurture in the "discipline and instruction of the Lord" (Eph. 6:4). And this pattern is recognizably present in both Old and New Testaments, even if the apostle Paul type of dramatic conversion and baptism usually receives more prominence in much of popular Christian consciousness.

The nurture model is already commended in Deuteronomy. "And these words which I command you this day shall be upon your heart; and you shall teach them diligently to your children, and shall talk of them when you sit in your house, and when you walk by the way, and when you lie down, and when you rise" (Deut. 6:6-7). Samuel and Jesus are examples of this nurture in faith. Paul too, as we have noted, counsels the Ephesians to nurture their children this way.

The apostle Paul elsewhere also acknowledges the special position of children of believers. Arguing in his letter to the Romans that salvation comes not by Abrahamic descent, he nonetheless asks, "Then what advantage has the Jew?" and replies, "Much in every way." For to them are "entrusted . . . the oracles of God" (Rom. 3:1-2). So Paul considers Jewish descent a special privilege. At the same time Paul immediately argues that it is *only* that—a privilege, not an automatic possession of grace. Ultimately, Paul argues, it is the children of faith who are the children of Abraham (Gal. 3:7). Paul therefore warns against drawing unwarranted conclusions from the Abrahamic promise. Nevertheless, it is a great advantage to be born and reared within the household of God.

In his letter to Timothy Paul expresses appreciation for the faith of Timothy's mother Lois and of his grandmother Eunice. As a consequence, says Paul to Timothy, "Continue in what you have learned and have firmly believed, knowing from whom you learned it and how from childhood you have been acquainted with the sacred writings which are able to instruct you for salvation through faith in Christ Jesus" (2 Tim. 3:14-15).

As already noted, the children of Christians are not biologically different from the children of non-Christians, nor even different in their early spiritual status. But the Christian community does provide a different environment, different relationships, influences, and usually (in the great majority of instances) a different spiritual outcome. So we can and should expect most of the children of Christians to become Christians themselves. One would need to charge culpable negligence if it were not so. For the Christian church is an incomparable setting for Christian witness and evangelism, offering as it does the opportunity of sustained communication of the heritage of faith to children and youth.

From what has just been said it might be inferred that if the New Testament pattern of baptism bespeaks someone's crossing over from sin to righteousness through redemption, and if children of the church are to be spared this service of sin through nurture within the community of faith, then children growing up in the church, like Israelites who grew up in the Promised Land, do not need any baptism at all.

For better or for worse this option has not been entertained seriously in the history of Christianity. To require baptism of descendants of Christians has been the almost unanimous impulse and normative practice of all branches of the Christian church throughout history (with the exception of minority groups such as the Salvation Army and the Quakers). This impulse has a sound basis, for there is a common denominator of meaning in the baptism of an adult convert from paganism and of someone nurtured within the church. In both instances, baptism calls for the appropriation of faith. Personal faith is not hereditary.

The justification of the church as a new community alongside of ethnic Israel is precisely its claim to existence and identity on the basis of actual faith and spiritual life, not on the basis merely of birth or ethnicity. It is therefore not inappropriate to make baptism a regular requirement even of people born and reared within the church. They ultimately become or remain members of the body of Christ not merely by virtue of their birth but only if they themselves actually appropriate its spiritual life. We could also add that if the church discontinues baptism, it will surely create a substitute to signify what baptism stands for, as pedobaptists have done in the rite of confirmation. The question, then, is not whether the church will administer baptism to its descendants, but when and how it will do so.

Why does the one model of baptism tend to dominate the pages of the New Testament? Proponents of infant baptism have tried to draw attention to the special circumstances of the apostolic period. Because most if not all of the first members of the Christian church were adult converts coming over from Judaism or Gentile paganism, the problem of baptism of second-generation Christians had not yet arisen or at least did not occupy front stage. If there were children of Christians coming to adulthood in the period of time covered by the book of Acts, for example, the New Testament nowhere discusses their situation. We must admit that we are left with a gap here and will need to find guidance from theological principle in the absence of explicit precedent or unambiguous texts.

Reinforcing the New Testament Model

The dominant New Testament pattern of baptism—that is, the baptism of adult converts—tends to get accentuated by Christians of the believers church tradition (and the alternative possibilities correspondingly ignored) because of several powerful factors in church history. Most basic of these is the Reformation and the Protestant principle of the authority of Scripture for faith and practice. Thus the New Testament, especially the Acts of the Apostles, is assumed to be a direct and even exclusive example for today's church life. Not much consideration is given to its unique historical setting.

Then, also, the New Testament pattern has been underscored by the Radical Reformation movement, in which converts came over from the Catholic Church into believing congregations just as converts in the New Testament came from Judaism and from the Greco-Roman world into the emerging Christian church. This again reinforces the New Testament pattern in the minds of people in the believers church tradition.

In modern church history the New Testament pattern gets reinforced by the modern missionary movement, in which converts from Hinduism or Shintoism or African religions cross over into Christian faith, again reduplicating for modern Christians the scenes from the Acts of the Apostles.

Finally, the New Testament pattern has been reinforced in the thinking of many Christians by the modern evangelistic movement of Western (especially Anglo-Saxon) Christianity, in which the preaching of the gospel has won "trophies of grace"—notorious characters such as Billy Sunday—who were converted as adults and demonstrated a notable transformation of life, once more reminding people of scenes from the Acts such as the conversion of Saul-Paul and the Philippian jailer.

Often the dramatic and sensational adult conversion pattern of baptism is assumed indirectly by what preaching and teaching in the church and Christian homes selects, ignores, emphasizes, or idealizes. Though implicit or only implied, such suggestion is nonetheless effective. In this vein Sunday school lessons emphasize the conversions of Zaccheus, Cornelius, Paul, and the Philippian jailer. Often the church conveys the impression that its most important program is overseas missions. Missionaries obtain education and training and are salaried for their work overseas. And returning missionaries are the heroes who report the gratifying salvation of the "heathen." The most exciting church rallies are those billing a former street-gang fighter or drug addict or political scoundrel or entertainer-turned-preacher. Such personalities are adulated and lionized, again because they seem to exemplify the pattern of the New Testament. And so often they also seem to be able to make a lot of money!

But when it comes to finding someone to teach Sunday school or to direct the youth fellowship, the congregation is too often satisfied with someone without training, without experience, and who will do his or her work on marginal time without financial support. No matter, this after all involves only the church's children and youth!

Sometimes parents even wish secretly that their children could have a clear-cut and decisive conversion like those sensationalized in the popular religious press, a conversion that marks a critical turnaround in life, offers assurance of salvation, and yields a gripping testimony.

Children and youth of the church get the message. Conversions of big sinners are, if not the only ones that count, at least the most important. Therefore one's task is to have a dramatic experience, maybe even do enough requisite sinning to make such a conversion highly credible.

Add to all this what proponents of believers baptism see in church history as the bad consequences of infant baptism, and there has developed an unfortunate oversimplification. Advocates of believers baptism have lost sight of the different situation of children of the church and have attempted indiscriminately to impose the dominant New Testament pattern upon everyone.

Imposing the New Testament Model

Because of their idealization of the New Testament pattern of conversion and baptism, Christians of believers baptism persuasion attempt, perhaps unconsciously, to impose that pattern upon their children and youth. There are essentially only two general ways this can be done.

The first way is to encourage youth to postpone the decision of faith to post-adolescence, or adult life. Young people are encouraged to sow at least some "wild oats," to pass through at least a brief period of estrangement from the church and its faith, in order to have something to be converted from and to demonstrate an authentic crisis conversion. As some readers will recognize, this pattern has been common in certain periods of Mennonite history.

The church may not explicitly demand a pattern of adult conversion in so many words, but social and religious precedent establishes the expectations. Accordingly the church fails to claim its youth at a timely age and resigns itself to seeing its youth enter upon a period of alienation and estrangement in order to qualify for what it considers a genuine break with the world, a New Testament type of conversion.

The tragedy, of course, is that some youth are permanently lost to the faith if they follow these expectations of spending a period of time in worldliness and sin. It is even a tragedy if they spend only a few years in the service of evil when it would be possible for them to avoid this by being so nurtured in faith as to move at the age of discretion directly into their own appropriation of the life of the kingdom.

Actually, most Christians, even if they idealize the dramatic conversion experience, would not choose such a pattern of life for themselves or for their children. If confronted with the choice, they would not wish for their children even a short season of estrangement from the Christian way as a price for one of those sensational conversions applauded on religious television.

Incidentally, the emphasis on conversion, while its intention is good, can have bad repercussions. It intends to summon people from the sphere of unfaith to the Christian way. But if addressed to people who have grown up *within* the Christian way, the demand for conversion tends to suggest a cross over into *another* tradition. That is why an unthinking demand for a dramatic conversion experience disposes some young people to convert to another religious movement or cult. We may be surprised at this and lament it, but our emphasis upon a dramatic conversion may have precipitated it.

It pays to be careful to press conversion only upon definitely non-Christian people. When it comes to young people of the church, our task is not to press conversion from one religious community to another but to encourage preservation of the heritage. For them we don't seek a cross over to *another* tradition, but appreciation and appropriation of the one they already live within. Their task is not to repudiate their past and present life in favor of a new community but to affirm the life of the one they already possess.

The second way of trying to impose the New Testament pattern of conversion and baptism upon children of the church is to demand a crisis repentance and conversion of children who are still innocent, still below the age of discretion. In this approach the church treats such children as culpable sinners, creates a sense of guilt in them, and artificially induces in them an adult type of experience of repentance and conversion. It is not difficult to induce this experience in innocent children, precisely because they are innocent and pliable and respond with what their elders expect of them.

In some forms of child evangelism this view of children as culpable sinners has become explicit doctrine. Children are considered accountable sinners, capable of making a willing commitment of faith on the classic pattern of New Testament conversions. Therefore a sense of sin is cultivated in them, and they are pressed to decide for Christ, though often the alleged conversion of children is not followed up by baptism, a sequence that consistency with the New Testament pattern would suggest.

This inconsistency, by the way, is already a telltale indication that something may be questionable about the so-called conversion of preadolescent children. Some well-intentioned believers baptism churches nonetheless unhesitatingly baptize children anywhere down to the age of five.

Attempts to get an adult type of conversion out of innocent children reflects to a great extent the influence of the American revivalist tradition. On the American frontier the majority of the population was non-Christian, and it was these adult unbelievers whom the evangelist preacher addressed at camp meetings. In recent years this rather heavy-handed evangelistic approach, appropriate enough in its original setting, was uncritically brought into an altogether different setting, the congregation. In this latter setting the only people not already full members of the church by personal decision and baptism were preteen children. So the hellfire preaching of the camp meeting was then directed at them.

There are indications that our churches have reservations about a simple and direct application of the New Testament model of baptism to the church's children. One is the already-mentioned practice of postponing the baptism of allegedly converted children until they are old enough "to know what they're doing"—that is, have reached the age of discretion. But violating the biblical pattern (which properly connects baptism with conversion) in the process of trying to impose the biblical pattern undermines the credibility of many claims for child conversions.

Another sign of the problems caused by attempts to impose the New Testament model of conversion and baptism upon innocent children is the appearance of second and even third "decisions" of faith by young people of our church, evidence that many of them were pushed into early "decisions" or premature conversion experiences—and also baptism—only to discover later that these were spurious. That discovery by young people then fosters skepticism about the authenticity of subsequent decisions as well.

Celebrating the Better Way

Let's face it, and gladly face it, the situation of children of the church is different. The more effective the job that Christian parents and the church do of guiding their children into the Christian way, the less likely it is that these children and youth *can* have a dramatic conversion experience. We must learn not to lament this. Grateful as we are for every bum or skid row derelict who got "unshackled," we must learn to exult in the even more glorious testimony of Christians who grew up in a home where grace was said at meals, who were taken to church and Sunday school, and who joyfully embraced in adolescence and for all of their life thereafter the Christian way taught and modeled for them by the church.

Today as in most periods of the church's life the great majority of the church's members come from its descendants. And throughout its history most of the church's leaders were the products of Christian homes.

Defenders of believers baptism have often—rightly— pointed to the dangers of establishment Christianity, a religious status in which people were merely socialized and acculturated into nominal Christianity, lacking heart faith and true discipleship. These dangers cannot be ignored. No people are automatically Christians simply because their parents were but only because they themselves chose the obedience of faith.

The answer to this danger, however, is not found by disparaging second-generation Christianity. For what are first-generation Christians supposed to do? Refuse to rear their children in the nurture and discipline of the Lord? Make them pagans so they can be first-generation Christians? Unless we choose monastic celibacy or experience perpetual martyrdom in the church and consequently have no offspring, merely modest missionary success and the passage of time places in our hands the task of Christianizing our children. Since they are human beings too and the objects of God's love and grace as much as pagans are, we must accept our responsibility to minister to them as much as to the non-Christian world.

The total mission of the church involves both horizontal expansion and historical extension. By horizontal expansion I mean the church's outreach with the gospel to non-Christians in the world around it. Success in that task then entails the other task of linear extension—living out the implications of the gospel in family life and in Christian community, which calls for nurturing in faith the children and grandchildren of converts, saving them from entrance upon a period of life in the service of unrighteousness. Even if the whole world were successfully evangelized through lateral extension, the task of Christianizing children would continue.

The ultimate ideal of the gospel, we should remember, is not just a perennial salvage operation directed toward a lost humanity, but a consolidation and preservation of Christian communities from generation to generation so that children born into God's world can inherit their birthright—to grow up instructed in the knowledge and blessing of God's way.

So, then, whatever their criticisms of infant baptism, advocates of believers baptism must recognize the valid insight it points to. Birth within the covenant community carries a definite privilege. There is a difference between growing up within the boundaries of the church and under its influence and growing up outside it. There is a correlation, even if not complete, between birth within the church and personal appropriation of its faith.

What we have sketched in this chapter will be hard for some people in the believers church tradition to accept, given our biblicist emphasis and restitutionist impulse to reproduce the New Testament pattern of the church. We will need to concede, however, that the apostolic church pattern of adult conversions represents a special historical period and does not cancel or invalidate the other complementary biblical model of nurture within the community of faith. Though the story of salvation in many individual lives and geographic areas of the world may *begin* with the conversion of adult sinners, the crowning goal of salvation remains a totally redeemed human social order in which the nurture of children as well as all other dimensions of human existence are brought into conformity with the gracious purpose of God. Although it is never too late to present the gospel to unredeemed sinners, the best way is for people to be born into the family of God and to be nurtured in the faith and to personal faith within that family.

Chapter 4

ORIGINAL SIN AND ELECTION
Infant Baptism and Confirmation

It might be inferred that the line of thought just presented concerning the special situation of children of the church implies a concession to infant baptism. Proponents of believers baptism might even charge us with having completely capitulated. Pedobaptists will no doubt conclude that we have at long last come to see the light.

Infant baptism has been, we must admit, the most longstanding practice of the majority of churches throughout Christian history. Infant baptism has been their attempt to adapt the New Testament pattern of baptism to children of the church. But does the recognition of the special status of children of the church necessarily lead logically to infant baptism? We cannot here go into the long, interesting, and important story of the rise of the practice of infant baptism in church history. We can in a preliminary way observe, though, that infant baptism is not as monolithic, unchanged, and unchanging a practice as is sometimes alleged, even though Origen (who died in AD 254) claims the practice reaches back to the time of the apostles. Pedobaptism developed to a considerable extent by intuition, accommodation, and compromise, and therefore it has not always shown internal consistency, though its theology possesses a fundamental logic, as we will see.

The earliest unambiguous reference we have in history to a variation from the dominant New Testament pattern is in the Latin church writer, Tertullian (about AD 200). Even here we have to do, though, not with infants but with children, for Tertullian uses the Latin term "parvulus" and not the term "infans." Gregory of Nazianzus, a bishop of the early church (died in AD 390) defended the baptism of children, but he nevertheless set the age of three as a lower limit, for the reason, he says, that people should have some memory of the experience.

According to one writer infant baptism evolved by a continuing depression of the age of baptism until baptism merged with the ancient Roman rite of water-purification and name-giving of a newborn child.

> In the religious custom of the Romans the water of purification played an important part ... with newly born girls on the eighth day after birth, with boys on the ninth day, in order to protect them against sorcery. It was effected by the child being carried through the house to the household altar and even through the temple.... And on this day [they] received their *proenomen* [first name].[21]

It is noteworthy that despite Origen's claim about the practice of infant baptism reaching back to the time of the apostles, "in the old Christian families, whose members had been Christians for several generations," infant baptism was *not* observed. For example, Ambrose was baptized at the age of thirty-four, Jerome at twenty, Augustine at thirty, Gregory of Nazianzus at thirty, Basil after his return from the

University of Jerusalem, and Chrysostom after a three-year course of instruction.[22]

An examination of the subject suggests that behind all the rationalizations for the doctrine and practice of infant baptism—Jesus' blessing of the children, household baptisms reported in the Acts of the Apostles, the analogy with circumcision—there are in the end only two basic postulates for infant baptism: (1) baptism is needed to deal with original sin, and (2) infant baptism is called for by the fact of divine election indicated by birth within the covenant community. The first of these postulates is more characteristic of Catholic, Lutheran, and Anglican thought, the second of Calvinist or Reformed theology. The two are not necessarily correlative or mutually implicated, however, nor even fully consistent with each other.

The Argument from Original Sin

The original sin argument is not found in nearly all of the patristic briefs for infant baptism. Numerous church fathers, especially in the Eastern church, argue for pedobaptism on the basis of the innocence of children, not on the basis of original sin. For example, Chrysostom, bishop of Constantinople (died 407), says, "We baptize little children also, although they have no sin."[23]

The idea of baptism for original sin is mentioned already by Origen (about 185-254), who says, "By the sacrament of baptism the pollution of our birth is taken away."[24] But it was Augustine who gave the doctrine of original sin its systematic formulation, and it has maintained its force all through the ages until modern times.

The logic of the original sin argument is very simple. All children of Adam have inherited sin; according to the teaching of the New Testament, baptism saves from sin; therefore children should be baptized, the earlier the better, because if they are not baptized they will be damned.

A modern writer restates the argument thus: There are only two relevant questions, "whether infants should be regarded as under sin and whether baptism is effectual in cleansing from sin." Since the answer to these questions is presumed to be "yes," infant baptism inescapably follows. This proponent of infant baptism elaborates:

> The taint of sin.... though it is not expressed as conscious sin in little children ... is nevertheless there as a condition, an effect of the fall of man. This condition ... is sometimes called original sin.
>
> The need for an infant to be baptized is basically the same as for an adult.... Because of sin, there is need for cleansing, and baptism offers this cleansing.
>
> Those who deny infant baptism might as well say that infants have no need to be brought into a boat for safety from a threatening flood.[25]

In this, its simplest formulation, the argument from original sin attempts really to apply to infants—and without modification—the New Testament pattern of baptism. That is, the child is, like an adult, considered a sinful person, and baptism allegedly confers upon the infant repentance, forgiveness, the gift of the Spirit, regeneration, moral renewal, and everything else baptism typically signifies according to the New Testament when applied to an adult convert.

Such a claim for the efficacy of baptism is frequently labeled the doctrine of baptismal regeneration or sacramentalism. That is, it teaches that the act of applying water as such inherently conveys the salvation associated with baptism in the New Testament.

The original sin rationale for infant baptism can thus be seen to be merely an extension all the way to infancy of the practice noted in the preceding chapter of baptizing innocent children and yet pretending such an act to be a direct and unmodified application of the New Testament model.

There is a most intriguing implication of the original sin argument for infant baptism. According to the logic of this argument and the claim for the sacramental power of baptism to confer salvation, there is no good reason to restrict baptism to the children of the church. Indeed, this logic supplies powerful reasons for indiscriminate or promiscuous baptism, the church applying baptism to any and all children it can lay its hands on.

From the time of Augustine onward "baptism was now and again administered even to the children of non-Christian parents." Baptism was declared a benefit of which "one may not deprive such poor creatures." From time to time "Jewish children were taken away . . . by craft or force" for baptism.[26] At the time of the Reformation one Anabaptist writer asks what fault it was of the infants of Jews and Turks that they were not baptized![27]

Already by the time of Thomas Aquinas this policy of baptizing children of non-Christians was discouraged, however. Calvin flatly forbade it. Indeed, Calvin turned the matter around to insist that "nothing is more preposterous than that persons should be incorporated with Christ, of whom we have no hopes of their ever becoming his disciples. Where none of its relations present himself to pledge his faith to the Church that he will undertake the task of instructing the infant, the rite is a mockery and baptism is prostituted."[28] Almost all pedobaptists today would agree with Calvin.

We should note another intriguing point related to the original sin argument for infant baptism. This argument does not logically require any separate rite of confirmation of the sort widely practiced in Western Christianity. In earliest pedobaptist practice and in all of Eastern Orthodoxy till today confirmation has been one rite together with water baptism, and this one rite signifies the gift of spiritual life and full incorporation into the church. Imposing the New Testament pattern of baptism upon infants with little or no modification, the church has alleged that baptism brings infants fully within the sphere of salvation, hence nothing further is required at any subsequent time to complete the process of becoming a faith-full member of the church.

In Eastern Orthodox Christianity to this day baptized children receive the Eucharist. That the Eucharist has been withheld from baptized but not-yet-confirmed children in Protestant Christianity is a tacit admission that infant baptism is *not* really believed by pedobaptists to confer an owned faith.

In recent times even many pedobaptists have been calling into question several aspects of this classic doctrine: the idea of original sin itself, the notion that original sin renders unbaptized children reprobate, and the belief that infant baptism sacramentally effects the kind of salvation connected with the baptism of adults according to the New Testament.

Calvin claimed "that children who happen to depart this life before an opportunity of immersing them in water, are not excluded from the kingdom of heaven."[29] In reaction to the classic view about infant sinfulness and damnation, many pedobaptists today tend to argue just the opposite— that infants are innocent and *without* sin and therefore qualified for baptism on the ground that if baptism signifies the movement from sin to righteousness, then the innocent sinless child is supremely qualified for baptism.

In response to this reversed argument for infant baptism

on the basis of the innocence or sinlessness of children, we insist on noting that there is again no justification for discrimination against children of non-Christians. The argument calls for promiscuous baptism of all children the church can reach.

Having registered the foregoing strictures about the doctrine of original sin, we must acknowledge one valid and important insight it contains, even though it has accumulated so many unfortunate connotations that we encounter difficulty salvaging the term. According to biblical teaching there is an Adamic nature in all individuals of the human race that conflicts with the purposes of God. This selfish nature must be superseded by the nature exemplified in the servanthood of Jesus of Nazareth. Every person must learn to "die to sin" and to say, "Not I, but Christ" (Gal. 2:20). Every person must "have this mind among yourselves, which is yours in Christ Jesus" (Phil. 2:5), not the mind of Adam. Every person must "not be conformed to this world but be transformed by the renewal of your mind" (Rom. 12:2).

According to biblical thought original sin is not a given or fixed quantity of evil brought like a load of karma into the world by a particular soul at its birth, a quantity of evil that can be removed by some liturgical act or rite. The responsible way to achieve the replacement of the fallen human nature by the new nature of Christ is not necessarily to baptize infants but to provide children and youth with the requisite example and teaching as they grow up so that they are enabled to receive the new nature of Christ in due time, especially when they reach the age of discretion in adolescence. Those who take original sin most seriously are not necessarily those who hasten children to the font, but rather those who nurture children and youth most effectively toward the actualization of the "not I, but Christ" form of life in which the dominating influence of the Adamic nature is broken by God's love and power, so that even if that original fallen nature is not totally removed, the Spirit of God becomes the governing power of an individual's life.

We conclude, then, that the argument from original sin is not an adequate justification for infant baptism.

The Argument from Election

The most basic and important rationale for infant baptism already in the past, but even more today, is not original sin but the doctrine of election. This view has been worked out most articulately in the Calvinist or Reformed tradition, but it has come to influence all branches of pedobaptism today, especially in North American Christianity. As one theologian puts it, "Infants have a right to the sacrament because they belong to the covenant people, or are heirs of the divine promise."[30] The central thesis of this election argument for infant baptism, as briefly stated in the foregoing chapter, is that in God's sovereign grace some children are privileged to be born and nurtured within the community of faith, the church. According to this view baptism does not so much represent incorporation of infants into the company of the redeemed as it signifies the fact that they are numbered among the redeemed already by birth. Thus, children of the church are not born in unfaith and given faith by baptism but are born and grow up within the community of faith, though they must in due time endorse or choose the life of faith for themselves when they reach independence.

Now the crucial question: if baptism, the rite we see practiced only in connection with adult converts in the New Testament, is to be applied to children who are born to members of the community of faith, at what point is it most appropriately applied, at their birth or at the time when they personally covenant faith?

Pedobaptists hold that on the covenant argument baptism should be applied at birth, because according to the New Testament pattern baptism signifies the beginning of the life of faith, and since the child is born within the community of faith, his or her life of faith actually begins at birth.

Proponents of believers baptism hold that baptism should be applied at a given person's own willing and responsible appropriation of faith. According to the New Testament pattern, baptism signifies the conscious decision of faith, and since this doesn't occur until an individual is able to make that decision upon reaching the age of discretion, baptism is properly applied only then.

We can concede that both of these answers are inherently compelling and appealing. On one reckoning it would seem that birth is the analogue of a convert's entrance into the community of faith. On another reckoning it would seem the true analogue is personal appropriation of covenant faith. Since there is no direct and unambiguous biblical precedent or directive to help us choose between them, we must make our choice on the basis of theological coherence and consistence.

My reasons for commending the believers baptism option begin with a review of the difficulties I find in the covenant pedobaptist position.

1. The development of the practice of infant baptism has been followed by the development of the rite of confirmation. It is not possible for us to trace here the long, interesting, and complex history of the development of this rite in Western Christian history.[31] We can only note that confirmation has come into its richest and fullest meaning in the

framework of Reformed theology, because confirmation functions there as a needed complement to the doctrine of birth-election. Natural birth within the community of faith is an immensely important act of divine grace, as it provides opportunity for instruction in the gospel. But such instruction remains of little value if it is not followed by personal ownership of covenant faith. Confirmation, then, becomes just as important and decisive as birth, if not more so. As the development of confirmation shows, applying baptism to infants requires the creation of a new rite to perform the function of signifying that faith has been personally appropriated.

In its strict definition—and also according to its historical origin—confirmation is the conferring of the Holy Spirit on a confirmand. In less sacramentalist terms, confirmation signifies that a confirmand has received or is receiving the Spirit. In any case, the laying on of hands in confirmation identifies an individual as a recipient of spiritual life.

In New Testament and earliest patristic baptism, such confirmation was part of one whole baptismal rite. The separation of confirmation from water baptism demonstrates that while a baptized child is considered a member of the Christian community by the application of water, such a child only later at confirmation enters for himself or herself upon an accountable Spirit-endued life.

The pedobaptist tradition is to be commended for not leaving a deficiency here. Having adopted infant baptism, it properly recognized the need for a decision of faith later by youth of the church. Luther was inclined to scrap the sacrament of confirmation on the grounds that it was a Catholic tradition and could not be justified from Scripture. Protestant continuation of confirmation despite Luther's opinion about it should perhaps be an embarrassment to pedobaptists, because confirmation as practiced today is a church tradition not found in Scripture.

As we have seen, there is good reason for the emergence and continued use of confirmation in pedobaptist churches. But one cannot help asking what is gained by applying the New Testament rite of baptism to infants, only to create a surrogate baptism to fill the void left by this transfer. Besides, there is available already since pre-Christian Jewish times a worthy rite of infant dedication to express the significance of birth within the covenant, a rite of thanksgiving and recognition of the special status of the child as well as parental-communal commitment to the task of nurturing the child to faith.

Some recent Anglican discussion would see in confirmation not the development of a new sacrament but the division of one original sacrament into two halves separated by a dozen or more years. Infant baptism then becomes the first half of the sacrament and bespeaks the privilege of election and the offer of God's grace addressed to the child. Confirmation becomes the second half, representing the acceptance of grace, the response to God's offer.

Anglicans, often enamored of tradition, have been understandably bothered by this fracture of what is in the New Testament and patristic church one whole sacrament. The pressure seems to be either to confirm the baptized child at the time of baptism, as the Greek Orthodox Church does, or to baptize at confirmation. Now the classic definition of a sacrament (as we noted in chapter 2) is "a sign and the thing signified." On this definition one should choose the second option of baptizing at confirmation, because the *substance* of the sacrament, the thing signified, is faith, and that is precisely what the appropriation of faith by the confirmand signifies.

2. A second problem in covenant pedobaptism is its equivocation on the status of children in the time between baptism and confirmation. In the Greek Orthodox Church, baptized children are, of course, considered full members. In the Methodist Church baptized children are called preparatory members. In general, Protestant pedobaptism vacillates between the claim that infant baptism anticipates faith and the claim that it bespeaks the infant's present and actual possession of faith.

While some pedobaptists might claim full possession of faith for baptized children, most of them would reply that infant baptism is really only anticipatory. It is the first stage of a process of nurture that results in confirmation. If that is the case, then one must observe again that baptism is not very appropriately applied to children. For baptism in even its most general New Testament meaning does not signify merely the likelihood or hope of a person's becoming a believer in the future, but of that person's actual entrance into the life of the Spirit.

A sensitive issue with respect to the status of baptized children is the question of their eligibility for communion. Paul Jewett has recently drawn attention to the ambivalence of pedobaptists on this question. As Jewett notes, most Protestant pedobaptists deny the need of faith in an infant as a condition for baptism. Yet they insist on faith as a condition for participation in communion, thus withholding communion from baptized but not-yet-confirmed children,[32] though some pedobaptist churches are now permitting or even encouraging the participation in communion of such children.

My point here is that pedobaptist equivocation on the *real* status of baptized children revealed by this communion issue suggests that baptism is not the best way to recognize the special position of children of the church. If baptism in the New Testament signifies incorporation into full membership, then to apply the rite to infants claims too much. Baptism should preferably be applied where full incorporation occurs.

Such a policy in no way implies lack of appreciation for the doctrine of election or lack of concern for the nurture of children of the church, as the life of most believers baptism congregations amply shows.

3. While on the one hand the covenant rationale for infant baptism shows ambiguity and equivocation on the status of children between baptism and confirmation, on the other hand it tends to draw a too sharp and contrasting line between baptized and unbaptized children. Although most Protestants have abandoned the Augustinian position on reprobation of unbaptized infants, there nevertheless remains an unfortunate connotation that baptized children are saved whereas others are not. It could hardly be otherwise as long as baptism is alleged to signify what it does in the New Testament (salvation) and the rite is then applied to infants.

This problem has bothered churches that practice infant baptism and prompted many of them to be more and more inclusive in their admission to baptism. But seeing the consequences that such indiscriminate baptism leads to, many have concurred with John Calvin in the remark already noted that "nothing is more preposterous than to baptize those of whom we have no hopes of their ever becoming disciples."[33] In the end, then, Protestant pedobaptist policy tends to admit to baptism only children with at least one Christian parent (or Christian guardian), which returns us to the prejudicial suggestion that the children of a Christian parent are saved, others not.

The almost unavoidable suggestion of baptism as the

great divide between saved and reprobate children leads to several unfortunate consequences. For one thing it can encourage a measure of complacency in the nurture of baptized children on the assumption that they already possess salvation by reason of their baptism. Where it is taken for granted that they will identify with their parents' faith, confirmation frequently becomes quite perfunctory. For another thing, it can encourage Christians to resign themselves to the expectation that children of non-Christians will become non-Christians. Natural generation becomes accepted as the governing principle of spiritual identity and status.

The truth is, life is not that tidy, and the lines cannot be drawn that sharply. A whole welter of factors enters the mix and intrudes upon the principle of biological descent, important as that factor is. Strong Christians, weak Christians, divided families, Christian homes that neglect nurture, neighborhood influences, school relationships, television, clubs—all of these in the end play their role and add up to make the increasingly independent adolescent and young adult choice much more decisive than the ethnography of birth. A Christian neighbor can be a more determinative influence in the Christianization of a child from a non-Christian home than professing but neglectful Christian parents are in the nurture of their own children. It therefore behooves the church not to let natural descent prejudice the case but to make the whole world of children an object of urgent outreach with the message of the way of Christ so that as many as possible may be brought in due time to a personal ownership of the way of faith.

4. Moving the rite of baptism to infancy involves too extensive a modification of its meaning. We noted earlier that the experience of children of the church appropriating the

faith in which they were nurtured is different from that of adult converts coming over from the world of paganism and unfaith. To baptize children of the church *either* in infancy *or* in adolescence or young adulthood is therefore a modified application of the New Testament rite of baptism, as we earlier explained. This fact has been recognized by proponents of infant baptism, but it has not often enough been recognized by proponents of believers baptism.

W. F. Flemington, a British advocate of infant baptism, admits to a measure of modification when he says:

> Many of the difficulties about the doctrine of baptism arise because statements . . . in the New Testament about adult baptism as they knew it in the first century A.D. are applied, without modification, to infant baptism as most Christian communions know it today. . . . It is obvious that the most characteristic New Testament baptismal teaching, originally formulated with . . . a reference to . . . adults, must undergo some measure of restatement before it can be applied to a situation . . . of . . . an infant.[34]

In a sense, then, the decision on whether to baptize in infancy or at the point where a youth of the church enters into an owned faith is a judgment call. As we have seen, both positions possess their own logical force. In essence those holding to believers baptism claim, however, that their adaptation of the New Testament model to youth of the church remains closer to the New Testament model in meaning and content. One Protestant writer, while supporting infant baptism, nevertheless goes so far as to suggest that "infant baptism is fundamentally a quite different sacrament from adult baptism."[35] In infant baptism "we are in the presence of a new sacrament."[36] In the New Testament the central element is response to the call of the Spirit. But this is not what is occurring in the infant, nor in the parents. They are committing themselves to nurture of the child in the Christian way so that he or she will in due time respond to the call of the Spirit. The occasion of that response, usually recognized in confirmation, is then the most appropriate moment for the application of water.

Proponents of infant baptism may claim that withholding baptism from infants implies lack of appreciation of their position, failure to acknowledge properly God's elective grace, perhaps even neglect of nurture of children of the church. The decision against infant baptism does not, however, imply a lack of concern for the salvation of children of the church. It does not imply neglect of their nurture. It does not lead to any lessened appreciation of their special situation. And it does not devalue their responsibility to appropriate their spiritual heritage for themselves.

The decision against infant baptism does not mean believers baptism churches have no problems. They too must deal with the question of whether their children should participate in communion. They must wrestle with the questions of how to make the appropriation of faith authentic and of when to baptize.

But when all is said and done, proponents of believers baptism are convinced that if the New Testament pattern of the baptism of adult converts is to be adapted to descendants of the believing community, there is less distortion of the New Testament meaning of baptism and there are fewer problems when baptism is applied to signify the act of owning the faith (usually in adolescence) than when it is used to signify natural birth into the community.

Mutual Influence

We have taken a rather sustained look at the doctrine and

practice of infant baptism because it is important for believers baptism churches to understand this position—for two reasons.

First, proponents of believers baptism have too often simply disparaged infant baptism without understanding its basic cogency. They have often, sad to say, been so conditioned to condemn infant baptism that they have failed to appreciate the basic intention behind it. Infant baptism is a recognition of the special situation of children of the church, and no dialogue with pedobaptists will be very helpful until this fact is appreciated.

Second, the infant baptism tradition has influenced churches of the believers baptism tradition to a considerable extent, whether they have been conscious of it or not. There are reasons to suspect that Christians of believers church persuasion have been affected by both of the basic reasons for pedobaptism just discussed, namely the original sin argument and the election argument.

One finds many parents in nonpedobaptist churches who entertain fears that because of original sin their little children are not saved. Parents are disturbed by the "Would they go to heaven if they died?" question. Many parents would like to be reassured by some simple rite that would guarantee their preadolescent children's salvation. In the absence of such a reassuring rite, Christians who practice believers baptism have too often tended to consider their children unbelievers, unsaved, such notions being the cumulative effect of centuries of the Augustinian thinking pervading Western Christianity generally.

One also finds perhaps even more often parents with the opposite attitude, namely, the complacent assumption that their children are secure. Parents take for granted that their children are numbered among the elect by reason of privileged birth, that growing up within the atmosphere of the church will more or less inevitably Christianize their children—if they are not Christians already. Their children's appropriation of the church's faith may be considered a rather routine "confirmation" by way of the annual baptismal class; thus their youth are acculturated and socialized in values they are expected to accept as a matter of course.

When parents unconsciously accept such theology, the eventual consequence will likely be an ambiguous church membership. Because of their outward decency and conformity to the rules of the church, children of the church are not denied membership in the institutional, organized church, even if they do not possess heart faith or live a Christian life. As a result baptism too often becomes a sign, not of spiritual life, but only of ethnicity and social-moral respectability. This is one way in which churches that practice believers baptism may be covertly closer to infant baptism in mentality and practice than to true believers baptism.

On the other hand, the believers baptism tradition has also influenced the pedobaptist tradition. We often do not realize the extent of the impact of the believers church vision since the time of the Protestant Reformation and Radical Reformation—that is, the recovery of the notion of a believing community within the world and all that implies in the way of pluralism, separation of church and state, voluntarism, and freedom of religion. Only a minority of denominations in Christianity have carried this vision to its conclusion in believers baptism. But even those that have not moved to believers baptism have come a long way toward acceptance of the presuppositions behind it, as even a brief comparison with pre-Reformation Christianity, both East and West, shows. We should therefore not undervalue the extent of the influence of believers church thought despite the persistence of infant baptism.

The lessening of tension between believers baptism and infant baptism is not necessarily to be deplored. Each tradition has influenced and learned from the other. At their best the two traditions are not even all that far apart in actual practice.

In both traditions, first of all, children born into the church are welcomed as a gift of God that the church must receive with thanks and nurture for God's glory. In both traditions children are really considered part of the community of faith. And though one tradition celebrates their birth with baptism and the other with child dedication, there is little difference in the subsequent process of nurture.

Both traditions encourage family worship, and in both traditions children are nurtured in the church's faith. Whether Presbyterian or Baptist, Methodist or Mennonite, children go to Sunday school to receive instruction in the gospel.

In both traditions, again, when children come to puberty or adolescence they are invited to own the faith of the community in which they were reared. In both traditions the age of baptism or confirmation is sometimes depressed a little too much, and the rite may even become too perfunctory.

It would seem to the impartial observer that though the respective interpretations appear to be miles apart, there remains little difference in the actual configuration of these respective ministries to children and youth except for the point at which water is applied.

In both traditions, at least in parts of the world such as Canada and the U.S. enjoying separation of church and state, continued membership in the church is voluntary. If infant baptism confers membership, such membership is discontinued in the event of failure to confirm or in the event of apostasy—at least in the ideal. And the churches that fail to live up to this ideal are not only those of the infant baptism tradition.

In both traditions, finally, the church extends its concern to people besides its youth. Both engage in active missions to the non-Christian world at home and abroad and incorporate those who come to faith as the result of such missions, using the classic New Testament pattern of baptism.

The extent to which pedobaptist and believers baptism churches have converged in their pattern of bringing to faith children of the church goes far to demonstrate that both traditions have discovered the realities of a common task and similar answers to that task.

If there are so many commonalities in the life of infant baptism and believers baptism churches, where then lies the disagreement? Is it an idle dispute?

The Continued Choice

We have granted that the New Testament model of baptism of adult converts is modified when applied to the church's children or youth. The question is: which practice conveys more dimensions of the New Testament pattern and thus justifies its adaptation and use of the rite and of the term baptism? Do we use baptism to signify the event of natural birth or the act of confirming, owning the heritage, covenanting for oneself upon reaching the age of discretion?

The answer to this question does not indefinitely remain merely a judgment call or matter of taste. It tends to generate very practical consequences. We tend to end up with a different kind of church as a result of baptizing people at their appropriation of the covenant than we do as a result of baptizing infants. The abiding conviction of believers baptism churches merits repetition here: to baptize in infancy, and thus to make baptism parallel to the meaning and function of circumcision in the old covenant, fails to do justice to the new covenant intent of a community whose identity is defined not by ethnicity but by the Spirit, even if there can and should be a high correlation between natural and spiritual generation.

To reserve baptism for the event of actual faith-covenanting helps to guard this biblical definition of the nature of the church. It does so by making an owned faith itself the criterion of membership in the church, rather than birth, privilege, or even the prospect of future faith.

Now it is possible to claim that actual faith is also the criterion for membership in pedobaptist churches, provided confirmation and church discipline is carried out with integrity to ensure faithful membership. But it appears quite unquestionable from a review of how churches have developed historically that infant baptism tends toward inclusivist and undiscriminating membership. It seems harder to later put out those baptized in infancy than to define membership in the first place by a positive act of commitment in adolescence or early adulthood.

The inherent tendency of infant baptism seems to be the creation of a distinction between a visible and an invisible church. "Outward decency" (to use an old Calvinist term) is the condition of membership in the visible church, but this criterion does not yet necessarily signify faith and the possession of spiritual life. This doctrine of an invisible church thus tends to proceed from and reinforce infant baptism, though it is not a necessary correlative of infant baptism.

In conclusion, we must recognize the special privileged position of children of the church, and we must recognize that to require baptism of them will necessitate adapting the New Testament model of baptism to their situation.

But to recognize these facts does not lead logically to infant baptism. We can and must respect those who hold to infant baptism, and we must respect their decision on how to apply the New Testament model of baptism. But for us the pedobaptist logic and practice have inherent difficulties and undesirable consequences that are avoidable. To apply water at the act of owning faith seems to us a more valid adaptation of the New Testament model, one that permits us to appreciate the role of children and to care for them and one that proves more effective in preserving a believing church.

Chapter 5

INNOCENCE AND ACCOUNTABILITY

A Theology of Children

We noted in chapter 3 the difficulties in trying to impose the New Testament pattern of conversion and baptism without any modification on children of the church. But we have also claimed that there are more difficulties with the infant baptism adaptation of the New Testament model. What then is our alternative?

One of the weaknesses of the believers baptism tradition has been its neglect of a theology of the status of children. It has not necessarily neglected *children* because, as we have seen, the believers church has intuitively developed a program of nurture of its children and youth remarkably like that of pedobaptist churches. Nonetheless, single-minded adherence to the New Testament pattern of baptism has hindered the believers church tradition from giving attention to what we call the more excellent way. Adult conversion and baptism permits, and should lead to, the nurture of children in the way of the kingdom, thus sparing such children a period of life in bondage to evil from which they must then be converted to faith.

The believers baptism tradition has not, in other words, been ready to recognize that the baptism of second- and third- and thirteenth-generation Christians inescapably requires an adaptation of the New Testament practice of baptism of adult converts. And this need of adaptation is not to be deplored or merely conceded with reluctance or embarrassment but celebrated with joy and thanksgiving as the fruit of the New Testament pattern of baptism.

Do not blame me for introducing this complexity. Children are God's idea. He made them. And He has ordained not just their physiological growth but also the principles governing their psychological and spiritual development. When we stop to think of it, most of us would, as the creation account in Genesis does, pronounce God's creation good—with respect to children also. We cherish children. They are a universal treasure on God's earth, to be appreciated by all Christians as God's parable of salvation. He often uses them as an influence to remind humankind of the virtues of affection, responsiveness, guilelessness, and love. Our job then is not to counter God in trying to make sinners or saints out of what he has ordained to be innocent. Our job as a community of faith is to accept the task of becoming responsible stewards of this treasure, with all its potential, of innocent human life.

The Fact of Innocence

We must resist the temptation, then, to place the human race into only two classes, the saved and the lost. We are required to recognize also a third class, the innocent, though the innocent in the economy of God are vulnerable to influence, education, example, and environment, and at the age of independence move into one of the other two classes.

God has thus arranged his creation so as to make it possi-

ble for children to avoid altogether a period of life in the service of sin—if God's people accept this arrangement and
work with God's intention for children to be privileged to
take the more excellent way into faith.

Through the centuries up to the present, many people in
Christendom, even those in the pedobaptist tradition, have
not adequately respected the status of children. Christians
have tended to simplify God's order by collapsing the three
categories into two. Sometimes Christians have condemned
some or all children as though they were culpable sinners.
Often churches have neglected a nurture appropriate to
children, either because some of them were assumed saved
by virtue of infant baptism or written off as lost because of
the absence of Christian parents and baptism.

It is time for both traditions to rethink their theology of
children—or lack of it—and to bring church practice into
line with what is now increasingly recognized and is beginning to be articulated about "faith development" of
children.[37]

We have acknowledged that Calvinist covenant theology
has for some centuries drawn attention to the privileged
status of children born within the community of faith. But
covenant theology's refusal to baptize children who will not
be nurtured in faith indicates that *nurture* is really decisive,
not the accident of birth as such. (For example, in
pedobaptist churches adopted children are baptized.) Since
all children are born innocent, where they end up is heavily
influenced by their exposure in childhood, by whether or not
they are beneficiaries of godly training.

A Mission to Children

Let's be clear about the implication of this observation
about the importance of nurture. It is not that we should

baptize children of Christians but decline to baptize children of non-Christians. Instead we should try to reach as many children on earth as possible with godly nurture. We should see in every innocent child that God gives to humanity a fresh opportunity (at least in principle) for the more excellent way of nurture. Every child should be seen as someone that might be saved from entering upon a life of sin.

Too often the church (in both believers baptism and pedobaptist traditions) has offered Christian education to its children and youth but shown benign neglect of children and youth of the non-Christian world—only to turn around and launch missions and programs of evangelism to the adult non-Christian world. Evangelizing adult non-Christians is obviously needed, but wouldn't it make more sense to give more attention to a preemptive approach, to try to reach children of the world before they enter a life of sin?

I confess that the church's responsibility to minister to children is one of the unexpected conclusions that has impressed itself upon me in this study of believers baptism, which has traditionally stressed "adult" baptism. But as I have indicated, believers baptism of the New Testament kind is *intended* to create churches and homes in which children can be nurtured to faith. Moreover, the church can and should seek to extend its nurture, example, teaching, influence, and ministry to as many children as possible.

I am not herewith advocating a return to the theology and methods of what is commonly called child evangelism. And I am not suggesting that the church is not already engaged in an outreach to children. But the church does not often appreciate enough or put enough resources behind the many avenues of opportunity in children's clubs, camps, foster homes, big brother and big sister programs, as well as in the more traditional Sunday schools and youth fellowships, perhaps even the "bus ministry" carried on by some churches.

While a Christian appreciation of children shouldn't lead to the invidious discrimination of infant baptism (the inclusion of children of Christians and exclusion of other children) but to an effort to shepherd the God-given, world-wide treasure of children and youth, it is still legitimate to speak of children of the church. There are, to be candid, degrees of influence the church can achieve. There are children and youth among whom the church has free and unhindered access for nurture, and these are not always just the children of Christians. There are, of course, militant atheists and people of other faiths who resist Christian influence upon their children.

It is thus appropriate to speak, even if relatively, of children of the church whom the church is able to take under its care. The expression, "children of the church," is to be preferred to "children of Christians." For though there will be a heavy correlation between "children of the church" and "children of Christians," we must make room for the broader scope. As we have seen, faith is not genetically determined; not all children of Christians themselves ultimately choose faith, and children of non-Christians can certainly be nurtured in the Christian way. Moreover, the Christian nurture even of children of Christians is more than the influence of the home alone. It is a ministry of the church as a whole. Even pedobaptist churches have in their recent theology urged churches to make infant baptism not just a family rite but a congregation-centered act, the total congregation's commitment to a child's nurture.

Christian nurture involves more than mom and dad. The whole church is involved. Many Christian parents have been thankful they did not have to do it alone, that they had the help of Sunday school teachers, youth ministers, a pastor, and Christian neighbors to provide role models of Christian life and to offer breadth and reinforcement to their own efforts in Christian teaching.

All of this is not to minimize, certainly not to demean, the role of Christian parenthood. Such a role remains a preeminent factor in a child's life, just from the sheer amount of time it occupies and the psychological impact it makes, especially in preadolescent years. All who would be genuinely Christian parents should take heart and work at the skills needed to structure Christian homelife in all of its dimensions—worship, discipline, learning, work, and play.

And yet Christian "parenting" always remains an extension of the church. We must recognize the correct order here. While there is a reciprocal relationship between the biological family and the spiritual family, the spiritual family remains primary. The biological family does not produce the spiritual family, nor does the spiritual family simply coincide with the biological family. Rather, as the example of Abraham already shows, the call of grace and gift of faith that creates the spiritual family also thereby makes Christian the biological family (in those who are called to married life), just as it creates Christian business, Christian medical care, and Christian programs of education.[38]

It is appropriate, then, to speak of the Christian family, which really is an extension of the family of God into the home, since Christians do not cease to be Christians when they return from gathered worship to their homes. And the family setting should be used to nurture spiritual life.

It is important for us to grasp two main implications of the theology just sketched of the place of children in God's economy. First, recognition of the innocence of children calls for an appropriate program of religious education and respect for what one writer has aptly called the religion of childhood. Second, the recognition of a transition from innocence to the age of discretion or accountability calls for serious effort to understand and respect the dynamics of this transition and to use the best resources of the church to coach youth into an authentic ownership of the heritage in which they were brought up.

The Religion of Childhood

Honoring the God-ordained innocence of children does not imply cheerful neglect of their religious education, as though they could grow up like wild creatures of nature. The church is responsible to fulfill its task of nurturing its children and youth toward faith—of nurturing all children and youth toward faith, as far as this is possible. At the same time the church should not assume that children are capable of an adult understanding of the way of faith or of an adult response to it.

What kind of teaching is appropriate to innocent children? It should be a teaching about Christianity, about God and salvation history, but with a different approach and application than that used with an accountable person of unfaith or with an adult believer. We cannot expect young children to grasp all the meaning of the cross as suffering love, of the truth of our death and resurrection with Christ, of love for the enemy, of repentance and grace.

By the same token we should not expect young children to achieve an adult grasp of the meaning of sin and guilt. We should not, therefore, try to create in them an adult conscience. The pressure of revival meeting preaching is often an unhealthy influence upon children, especially the kind aimed at producing conviction of sin in adult unbelievers. Such manipulation of children into guilt is one of the bad features of some evangelism directed toward children. It inculcates an unhealthy "conviction of sin" that cannot be true conviction because the child does not possess the requisite growth in understanding and psycho-spiritual development to handle the idea or the experience. Spurious guilt feelings lead then to a spurious understanding of repentance and forgiveness. We end up with spurious Christian experiences, which then may take long, difficult counseling to straighten out. We need not miseducate our youth this way. We have open to us the opportunity of more adequate methods and approaches.

To my observation most churches and church agencies are doing an effective job of producing religious education materials appropriate for children at various levels of development. Educators in both pedobaptist and believers baptism traditions, using the insights of psychology and education, are in substantial agreement about the nature of children and about the instruction and materials befitting them at various ages.

A ministry of religious education directed toward innocent children then creates what one writer calls the "religion of childhood,"[39] namely, the conceptions and expressions of religious feeling of which an innocent child or youth is capable. Thus children may be expected to speak of loving Jesus, of being sorry for doing wrong, or of wishing to serve God. These expressions need not be disparaged. Indeed, they should be appreciated, even while we recognize that they do not yet bear the marks of accountability.

Parents and the church must acknowledge two things simultaneously. Religious education of innocent children and youth is a serious and urgent task, essential as a condition of moving them toward faith. At the same time the innocence of children must be respected. Naughtiness or religious expressions of childhood must not lead parents or the church into concluding that the child is either reprobate or in possession of a responsible faith.

The religion of innocence—children responding to the teaching and example of faith on the level they are capable of—is not unlike their response in other areas of life. Children sometimes, for example, play wedding. But we do not confuse such play with real marriage. Nor do wise adults condemn such innocent play, because it is the product of wholesome family and community life and represents a legitimate part of a child's intellectual and psychological movement toward responsible adulthood.

Similarly wise Christians do not confuse an innocent child's responses to the life and teaching of the community of faith with responsible adult faith. Indeed, the task of Christian adults is to help to structure responses appropriate to children and not explicitly or implicitly try to elicit adult responses prematurely.

Part of the religion of innocence is childhood disobedience and feelings of guilt. Christians should not, of course, neglect discipline of children but should teach them moral values and good conduct. Still, naughty acts or the tokens of a guilty conscience should not be taken as signs of reprobation. It bears repeating that the fears of many parents about the salvation of children who die in innocence are the product of an Augustinian doctrine of original sin and not of a biblical theology of children.

As already said, children are God's idea. He made them. And with the Bible we can say that the way God created things is good. So let us work with God, not at cross purposes with him. He loves our children at least as much as we do. He will do his part, as we must do ours, to bring the children we seek to nurture to an owned faith.

The Age of Accountability

We come, then, to the subject of the transition from innocence to independence. A corollary of innocence is the fact of accountability. Whatever the complexities of identifying it, we are obliged to recognize its reality. Pedobaptist churches recognize it in the practice of confirmation, as we have observed. Judaism has its "bar mitzvah," or "bas mitzvah," when a child becomes a "son" or "daughter" of the law. Secular society makes a definite distinction between juveniles and adults in courts of law. It establishes a minimum age for marriage. It protects children through child labor laws.

And most primitive societies have, anthropologists tell us, their puberty rites (rites of passage) in which persons move from a childhood status to an adult role in society. In short, the consensus of experience and the wisdom of the entire human race establishes what theology has usually designated an age of accountability, an age of spiritual and moral responsibility.

What is the age at which persons move from innocence into such accountability of moral responsibility? The evidence from anthropology and sociology—that is, the accumulated experience of many societies in history—points to adolescence. Adolescence is defined as "the state or process of growing up ... the period of life from puberty to maturity, terminating legally at the age of majority." Puberty is defined as "the condition of being in the period of becoming first capable of reproducing sexually, marked by maturing of the genital organs, development of secondary sex characteristics and ... by the first occurrence of menstruation in the female. The age at which puberty occurs (is) often construed legally as fourteen in boys and twelve in girls."[40]

It should be recognized that the actual age of accountability may vary from one individual to another. And the church in its ministry to youth will not be governed simply by an age established by society's law. We should recognize, however, that important as physiological-psychological developments are, social and cultural patterns affect the age of accountability as well. In a society in which youth are kept in school by law until the age of sixteen, cannot hold a job or get a driver's license until sixteen, cannot vote until eighteen, and are not usually allowed to live on their own until out of high school, we are deluding ourselves if we ask them to make authentic decisions with respect to personal faith at a much earlier age. We are also, of course, deluding ourselves if we presume to prolong the tutelage of adolescents indefinitely, for with the exception of abnormal instances of dependence, late adolescents will usually establish their independence regardless of what parents or society want.

I'm sure many people would want to put the age of accountability at a much lower age than the one suggested here. Such people will point to alleged conversions of many children at six, seven, or eight years, maybe even testify that they themselves were "saved" at such an age. Often, however, the very people who point to such early conversions do not expect them to be signed in baptism. One immediately recognizes an equivocation here. In the end adult control over when children or youth get baptized indicates the real situation. In fact, too often a child's alleged conversion is itself an extension of adult control over a child's experience.

Some people would hold that to place the age of accountability as high as we do here is to deprive children through several years of their life of the privilege of a relationship with God and to risk their being lost. The truth is, children are deprived of a relationship with God only if the church neglects appropriate nurture. If the church provides such nurture, children will have a relationship with God— the kind he has ordained. As mentioned above, there is a religion appropriate to children during the age of innocence. To refuse to recognize this leads only to forcing them into an artificial and inauthentic religious experience.

As we have already mentioned several times, the church's ideal for the youth it has under its ministry is to so nurture them that they can move directly from innocence to faith when they reach the age of accountability without going through a period of personal rebellion or alienation from the church. In this transition adolescents appropriate and affirm for themselves the faith of the community to whose spiritual life they have been exposed, a faith they have heretofore understood with only a childhood capacity.

The Transition to an Owned Faith

It goes without saying that the task of guiding youth from innocence to faith is a challenging and difficult one—though rewarding too. Often, however, the church has been lackadaisical in this task, not deploying its best energies or leadership talents here, perhaps because it takes the Christianization of its youth for granted.

The church cannot, of course, guarantee that all the children it ministers to will move into faith. It may be tempted to set up machinery to guarantee this result, but influences of the world and freedom of the will mean young people cannot be prevented from sometimes choosing to reject faith. In some cases the church may not be able to forestall an interim sojourn of youth in the world, or even prevent their ending up there permanently, tragic as this is.

If this occurs, the church must respect their decision even while it continues the offer of the gospel.

But such a sojourn in the world is not necessarily foreordained. It *is* possible to help youth move from innocence directly into faith. It is not necessary, in other words, to expect in every youth a period of rejection of grace, as some groups tend to assume. Believers baptism does not mean that someone has to be a big sinner before he or she is qualified to be saved. The only definitive qualification is *faith*. This implies, to be sure, an awareness of an alternative. And it is precisely a genuine personal choice, at the moment when youth become aware of the alternatives, not to choose the alternative of disobedience and alienation from God but rather obedience and identification with him. In theological terms, it is to choose with the second Adam rather than with the first. Jesus in his growth and choice is the model of this transition from innocence to faith.

Handling the transition from innocence to accountability in our youth seems to many people to be an almost impossible task. In one sense it is difficult. We must learn in the context of many detailed situations where to begin to give independence and responsibility, and how much to give. But some of the apparent difficulty arises because we haven't had clarity on the problem, not because the process is inherently that difficult. Seeking to bring to faith the children with whom we have had the advantage of a long and positive relationship is certainly easier than trying to convert someone in whom we must battle entrenched worldliness, sinful habits, or pagan patterns of thought.

Yet parents are tempted to "jump the gun," to get apprehensive before their children reach puberty. Fearful that their children might not make a decision for faith later, they maneuver and manipulate them to get them safely into the church while they still have control over them—that is, before their youth fully reach the age of moral-spiritual capability to make the decision of faith for themselves. We can pretend and even make it appear to be *their* decision when in fact it is one finagled by parental pressure.

Such tactics or strategies are abortive. They lead not to new births but to spiritual stillbirths. Though disguised, such methods are really forms of the same phenomenon we have in infant baptism but more harmful precisely because they are dressed up as believers baptism. In the course of my college teaching I have seen many young people who were baptized prematurely, who discovered a few years later the real meaning of spiritual life. Then, having been introduced to Anabaptism, they wondered whether they should be rebaptized, only to find that their church leaders, who lauded the Anabaptists for *their* courage to rebaptize, resisted following the example of the Anabaptists in this respect.

We don't need to push our young people into the church. We know that in the end our decision is not enough. They cannot live off their parents' faith but must realize a faith of their own. So getting them into the church prematurely is self-defeating. We can be assured that God in his infinite love desires the salvation of our children at least as much as we do. If so, it depends upon what God has to work with. That is, it depends upon how faithful we have been in teaching the faith to our children betimes, "When we rise up and when we lie down, when we walk by the way. . . ." If we do our part, God will do his. We can have a healthy confidence that he will call our youth in his own time and way. In the end there is no other way than to trust his Spirit (Jn. 1;14). When all is said and done, we shouldn't want it any other way than for them to encounter God and be encountered by him for themselves.

In due season the faithful teaching of the church will be used by God's Spirit to bring our youth to spiritual life. And where this occurs, there the church should be responsive and baptize. The church thus preserves the principle of an owned faith in the New Testament pattern of baptism and does not need to depart from it even in the case of its own children and youth. Owned faith is a felicitous term given currency in recent writings by John Westerhoff on the faith development of children, youth, and adults. It designates a faith people have made their own following a stage of searching, reflection, and self-conscious inquiry.[41]

The church should be careful to avoid making a simplistic correlation between baptism and any given age. Adolescent or adult discretion is a necessary but not sufficient condition for baptism. The sufficient condition is actual faith, which of course presupposes accountable status. We should therefore be unambiguously clear that we are speaking of believers baptism and not just of adolescent or adult baptism.

Baptism is intended to be, and should always remain, the sign of an owned faith. It will not do to fix the age of baptism of children of believers at some conventional age—for example, fifteen—as though that assures us of believers baptism. To make "adult baptism" the alternative to infant baptism suggests that it is still a given age that counts rather than the work of the Spirit and its fruit in awakening faith and spiritual life.

The entrance upon an owned faith in the youth of the church sometimes seems harder to discern than in a convert from the world. There may be no sensational turn-around in a Dave Yoder who grows up in the church as there was in a Nicki Cruz from the streets of New York. (You may recall the humorous story of the little five-year-old girl who sang in Sunday school, "Years I spent in vanity and pride. . . .")

Remember, however, that the church has the opportunity of close and sustained observation of its youth. Nor are we limited merely to passive observation and guesswork. Church pastors, teachers, elders, and parents can dialogue with the church's youth until they achieve clarity about their faith.

And what are the marks of true spiritual life? The marks of faith in youth of the church must be and will be what marks of Christian life are anywhere—love, humility, joy, peace of heart and mind, including peace with other people, freedom from the power of sin and fear and hate, righteousness, hope in God and in the future he controls, a readiness to fellowship with other believers, and a concern for the redemption of the world.

The church need not compromise when it comes to the faith of its youth, expecting in them a faith inferior to that of a convert from the world. There are not two kinds of faith, one kind in a convert and a second kind in someone who grew up under the nurture of the church. There is only one kind of faith, the kind depicted in the New Testament. The decision of faith by a youth of the church may not be expected to show the dramatic contrast of a converted adult. But the confession of faith still includes all the dimensions sketched out in chapter two: discipleship of Christ, the life of God's Spirit, commitment to the church, and moral probity. We need not settle for a second-rate faith in second-generation Christians, even though we may be tempted to accept acculturation, socialization, and social conformity as substitutes for genuine faith. At the same time we should remember that the church is looking only for spiritual life, not necessarily for spiritual prodigies. But where it finds spiritual life, the church should eagerly seek to guide such life to maturity.

Because the espousal of faith by someone who grew up in the church usually does not show the contrast of an adult non-Christian's conversion, the church is in danger of not appreciating this less sensational act of covenanting faith. The church may too often take for granted the decision of faith of its youth when in fact that decision represents for a youth just as momentous a step as a prodigal son kind of repentance and return from the far country.

For this reason it behooves the church to be serious enough to take time to celebrate the baptism of its youth in a way worthy of the importance of that event. Otherwise the act of covenanting may be depreciated in young peoples' eyes, causing them to feel uncertainty or even doubt about the importance and validity of their decision of faith. If the church does not recognize the significance of a youth's act of covenanting personal ownership of the Christian heritage, he or she may ask, "Since I came to church before my baptism and I continue to attend after it, what difference does my decision make?"

If the baptism of the church's youth is important despite its not being sensational, the church can offer practical recognition of the meaning of that step. It can take newly baptized members into the life of the congregation, sensing their gifts, offering them responsibility, and involving them in the mission of the people of God.

The point of this whole book is the importance of celebrating "the more excellent way"—the privilege of nurture of people within the community of faith and the opportunity of their avoiding a period of life in the service of sin. We must therefore reassure our youth that they are not being cheated out of some important blessing in bypassing the experience of the prodigal son.

We might remind ourselves that not all children and

youth of the church will necessarily fit the ideal. Not all will own their heritage in adolescence without some experience of alienation. Indeed, not all will inevitably accept the heritage of faith. We will see degrees of conformity to the ideal and therefore variation in the act of owning faith. When we do we can accept the realities of life without, however, encouraging alienation by adulating the prodigal son pattern.

Before this discussion is over we must return to the issue we have met before, the claim that in the case of children growing up in Christian homes or under the care of Christian churches the beginning of spiritual life is gradual. It is not necessarily always an immediate, datable, all-or-nothing proposition, but can be a process spread out over a period of time, perhaps over several months, sometimes even over several years. Isn't it incongruous to employ a datable baptism to signify this process? We might observe that this is no less a problem in confirmation.

I think we must concede that entrance upon an owned faith is often a process. We are creatures of history, and God deals with us in the course of time. No event takes place in an absolute instant. Even apart from this observation we must recognize gradual development as an inherent characteristic of adolescence. And if adolescence is not instantaneous, then the awakening of accountable faith may not be either. There may, in fact, be numerous instances where a young person does not even move smoothly from innocence to faith. He or she might move, in other words, through an interim of rejection of faith and *then* come to faith. Even apart from this, coming to faith may involve a considerable period of time.

But let us not overstate the problem of gradualness in coming to faith. There is a real sense in which sound teaching, the Holy Spirit's influence, and the operation of God's grace tend to crystallize Christian experience. Faith has a self-clarifying, self-strengthening way of working. That is, an insight in faith, be it ever so faint, leads to further insight in faith, so that if faith can function unimpeded in a normal way, it moves with purpose to clarity and fruition. If so, we should hope to avoid situations in which persons look back over a long period of their adolescent and even early adult life and can't recall coming to clarity in faith during that whole time, even if they are reasonably sure they are Christians now. Where that happens, we suspect that there was some hindering circumstance or deficiency in guidance, counsel, and Christian instruction.

The cases of persistent uncertainty aside, how do we deal with the transitional, gradual nature of even healthy beginnings of spiritual life? I know of no other way than to listen to the guidance of the Spirit and to baptize when Spirit bears witness with spirit and we recognize genuine spiritual life. The challenge before us is therefore to locate the act of baptism most nearly and most fittingly at the spiritual experience it signifies.

On this matter of timing, the church's baptism of its believing youth must improve upon the conventional pattern of annual baptism classes many believers baptism churches have adopted, perhaps in imitation of pedobaptist confirmation classes. Such routinized processes do not sufficiently recognize the extent to which the realization of an owned faith *can* be dated. One can't help but wonder whether a crop every spring is how the Spirit moves.

The importance of keeping baptism connected with the act of covenanting faith can be illustrated from an analogous situation in marriage. Imagine an arrangement of annual group weddings in our churches. Apart from the failure to recognize the specialness of each couple's experience, such

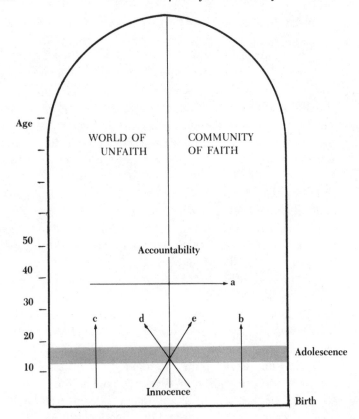

a. The New Testament pattern: adult converts come through baptism from the world of unfaith into the community of faith.

b. Children of the church are privileged to be able to move from innocence into an owned faith upon reaching the age of accountability without passing through a period of estrangement from the church.

c. Children who grow up under the influence of the world of unfaith tend to move into an adult life of unbelief.

d. It is possible for non-Christian influences upon children of the church to draw them into the world of unfaith.

e. It is also possible and most desirable for the church to reach out toward children of unbelievers and to bring many of them together with children of believers from innocence to faith without their going through a period in adult life of estrangement from the community of faith.

an arrangement would be ridiculous—and mischievous. Some couples might already be living together since January; others would not really be ready to live together until November. And yet all would be lumped together and married in June!

It is fortunate that usually we recognize timing to be of the essence in marriage. Marriage should take place at that point in time where a growing relationship between two people has prepared them to cross over from the single estate into the union of one flesh. We should observe the same principle in baptism, timing baptism to coincide with the emergence of an accountable faith.

Why is the correlation of baptism with emerging faith so important? Apart from this correlation being instinctively felt to be natural and right, a premature baptism would give someone false signals and false assurances, while delayed baptism would fail to give timely support and encouragement. A delayed baptism would also tend to suggest a second work of grace or new religious experience beyond the act of faith itself, with baptism removed from that initial act.

In baptism we ought to try not to run ahead of God nor to lag behind. We must be perceptive and poised to work with his Spirit, first in diligent nurture of children and youth in the church, and then in answering with baptism where he uses this nurture to awaken in them an owned faith.

We should reemphasize that for someone to grow up within the faith community does not obviate the need for conscious decision. We have noted that this decision is of a different kind than that of a pagan adult coming to faith. But many a transition to an owned faith will be forfeited if the church assumes that its youth will come to Christian confession and life more or less as a matter of course without some explicit summons or invitation.

There is a need in the life of the church then for opportunities or structured settings for youth to move to an owned faith. Traditionally evangelistic services or camp meetings or annual baptism classes provided these structured settings. We have mentioned the problem connected with evangelistic services and annual classes when used with children and youth of the church. But at least such services and classes provided opportunities for decision. If these activities are not carried on any more, then the church must work at creating others, else by default youth will not come to decision.

My inclination is to see the periodic gathered worship of the congregation as the best setting for the church to call its youth to decision. Perhaps the church should restore some creative adaptation of the periodic altar call. If not that, then some other effective opportunity for response must be found that is both appealing and impressive. Such an arrangement should not be bizarre, artificial, or awkward and thereby "turn people off." But at the same time the summons to decision should be sufficiently earnest—*and explicit*—to move youth to closure, to a decision duly signified in baptism.

The diagram on page 122 offers an illustration of the theology of children sketched out in this chapter.

Chapter 6

QUANTITY OF WATER AND TIME

The Mode of Baptism

We have said nothing so far about the proper mode of baptism because, as the discussion has shown, the *meaning* of baptism and the *when* are more important than the *how*. Indeed, the mode of baptism is to a considerable extent shaped by our conception of its meaning.

A review of the terminology concerning baptism in the New Testament and survey of early church practice (what we know of it) suggests that more water was usually involved in early church baptism than most pro-affusion people are content with. Yet in the absence of video tapes the immersionist argument cannot be pronounced conclusive. John the Baptist baptized where there was "much water." But the Acts of the Apostles doesn't specify concerning Paul, Cornelius, and the Philippian jailer. The New Testament apocryphal work called *The Teaching of the Twelve Apostles* speaks in favor of cold running water but settles for warm standing water where cold running water is not available. In the earliest churches of which we have archaeological remains (Italian basilicas), the baptistry was a free-standing structure near the church, and it contained a large masonry tank several feet deep. In the Greek Orthodox family of traditions baptism to this day is practiced by immersing infants in a large vessel.

Amount of Water

Evidence that early church baptisms involved the use of considerable quantities of water still is not evidence that they employed the forms of immersion maintained by Baptists or the Church of the Brethren today. While baptismal candidates at that time may well have washed or immersed all parts of their body at some point in the rite, there is no proof that they had all parts immersed simultaneously at one moment, as some immersionists would insist today.

If some moderns were actually to witness an apostolic form of baptism they might very possibly be shocked, for it seems that candidates at that time were baptized naked. From Jewish proselyte baptism to patristic baptisms in the third century, the ones we hear about are baptisms in which candidates removed all clothes and took a bath, symbolically cleansing themselves from the old life. Such baptisms were not, it is obvious, spectator events, though the *fact* of someone's baptism was usually public knowledge.

For over three centuries of its history the Anabaptist-Mennonite movement practiced almost exclusively baptism by affusion. Immersion seems to have begun with the British Baptists and spread from them back to the continent and to America and from there to other parts of the world. Shortly after their beginning in 1860, the Mennonite Brethren Church adopted immersion under Baptist influence.

If honest scholars differ on the biblical and historical data, how do we attempt to decide this question? Some writers suggest that ancient Middle East practices are inconvenient in our climate and culture. We should not decide this issue on the basis of mere convenience, though on that score our Baptist friends have made matters rather comfortable in their churches. A modern church historian writes:

> The trend through the centuries has been away from the early understanding which involved relishing, drowning in, and enjoying the water of life. The baptismal river became a pool; the pool became a well or cistern; the cistern became ... a font; the font became ... a bowl.... If the trend continues—perhaps it is not irreverent to ask—shall we soon be experiencing the waters, the Flood, the Red Sea, the Jordan, the water of life in the miniscule antisepsis of an aerator, an atomizer, or a humidifier?[42]

We must try to look at meaning. Yet here too the symbolism is manifold. Immersion, it is usually said, symbolizes death and resurrection with Christ, affusion the pouring out of the Spirit. Neither of these meanings is dispensable. Neither one is more important than the other. Indeed, they are mutually implicated and complementary.

Yet there is some force to the claim that immersion conveys a little more effectively than affusion the biblical imagery of Red Sea and Jordan, of radical "crossing over," even if, as early American Mennonites argued against the Dunkards, it was not redeemed Israel but Pharaoh's host that was immersed! In the debate of early American Mennonites with Dunkards, it is intriguing to see Mennonites in the unusual position of arguing from the Old Testament and relinquishing the New Testament to the Dunkards.

Often discussion of the proper mode of baptism pretends to be a learned and unbiased review of Greek lexical meanings of forms of the word *baptizo*, but it likely becomes in the end not a question of whether a given form is imposed upon us but of how perceptively we grasp the meaning of baptism and then shape our form to bespeak that meaning as adequately as possible. One writer conveys well the perception of the New Testament church. For its converts,

> The ... feet could never again be engaged on errands of hurt [or] ... mischief; the sexual organs could never again be devoted to lustful ... purposes, in fornication and adultery—they also had been baptized; the hands could never again minister hurt to any of God's creatures; the mouth could never again lend itself to false speech, whether lascivious, covetous, or malicious; the eyes could never again look upon evil with pleasure; the ears could never again listen to slander and false evidence and take pleasure in it; and the brain could never again devise schemes of craftiness and terror.[43]

The momentousness of baptism is conveyed also in a modern story, that of a soldier in the South Pacific in World War II who got converted and came to the chaplain for baptism. "I want to be immersed," he said. "God knows I got dirty all over, and I want to get clean all over." We are well aware, as Peter's epistle reminds us, that baptism is not a washing away of "dirt from the body" (1 Pet. 3:21). Nonetheless, this convert sought a mode of baptism that expressed as clearly as possible the total transformation of life he had experienced.

Amount of Time

A more important consideration than quantity of water in baptism is quantity of time. There are too many "quickie" baptisms which may employ immersion but move people through the baptistry at the end of a Sunday morning service in scarcely sixty seconds. In our Mennonite churches too we hardly do justice to the grace of God and to the value of someone's commitment of faith by taking only a few minutes out of a church service to process a half-dozen candidates. In the absence of a service commensurate with the momentousness of baptism, we should not wonder that much of the meaning and importance of it is lost upon our candidates and that they may come to take baptism as only a trivial event in their lives.

Our congregations do not make weddings ten-minute interludes in the service. Doesn't someone's crossing over into spiritual life merit at least as much attention as marriage? Our congregations owe it to themselves and to every individual who in baptism accepts responsibility for the way of faith to take enough time to celebrate this act in a way that does justice to its importance. The small amount of time we take is an embarrassing revelation of our deficient appreciation of the kingdom of God, of the value of participation in the messianic community, and of the import of someone's taking up the life of the age to come.

We likely should not try to go back uncritically to the elaborate baptismal celebrations of the early church, but it is instructive to see how much time and rich symbolism they invested in the rite. An example is the description by Cyril of Jerusalem (315-386).

> First the candidates gathered in the vestibule of the baptistery and, facing west with outstretched hands, formally renounced the devil and all his works and pomp and service. Then, turning to the east, they said: "I believe in the Father, and in the Son, and in the Holy Spirit, and in one baptism of repentance." Going thence into the inner chamber, they took off their clothes and were anointed with exorcized oil. Then, one by one, they were led by the hand to "the holy pool of divine baptism," where after a second profession of their faith they were immersed three times in

the blessed baptismal water to symbolize the three day's bu-
rial of Christ. Next they received the post-baptismal chris-
mation, and after putting on white garments the
"neophytes" proceeded, carrying lighted tapers, from the
baptistery into the church where they were greeted with
psalm-singing and received their first Holy Communion.[44]

Churches should not resort to artificial gimmicks to try to
achieve rich baptismal celebrations but rather find natural
contemporary expressions. Moreover, it would be desirable
not to develop too much local idiosyncrasy but rather to
have conference or denominational guidance in shaping
good baptismal liturgy. Let us fervently hope that the
church will not permit baptism to go the way of weddings,
where too many couples bring their own peculiar view of the
ceremony and write their own private, sometimes out-
landish, services.

Quite a few Mennonite churches make room today for
both modes of baptism, affusion and immersion. Certainly
the church should receive people baptized under either
mode, whether or not it insists upon uniformity in its own
practice. It might be suggested, half-seriously, that while immersion is most fitting for adult converts, affusion may be
more fitting for someone who is born and reared within the
community of faith and appropriates its faith without ever
leaving the Christian community. Second-generation faith
does not, as pointed out earlier, imply second-rate faith. The
faith of a second-generation Christian is as genuine as that of
a first-generation convert and often richer, thanks to years of
nurture and preservation from the evil influences of the
world. Still, it might be worth considering two modes of
baptism to distinguish between the adult convert coming
from the non-Christian world according to the New Testament pattern and the descendant of the church, who is nur-

tured in its life and comes to responsible appropriation of that life at the age of discretion. Such a distinction may have the merit of helping us to appreciate the special status of children of the church.

Chapter 7

CONCURRENCE OF WATER AND FAITH

The Question of Rebaptism

The question sometimes arises about the permissibility or even necessity of rebaptism. Such a rebaptism may seem required by the inadequacy of a prior baptism.

There is one reference to rebaptism in the New Testament. According to Acts 19:1-7 Paul and his party came upon a group of people at Ephesus who had received John's baptism. When Paul asked, "Did you receive the Holy Spirit when you believed?" they replied, "No, we have never even heard that there is a Holy Spirit," whereupon Paul expounded to them the whole counsel of God and rebaptized them.[45] There may be biblical justification, then, for rebaptism where something *called* a baptism is recognized by the church to have been unquestionably *not* a true Christian baptism—that is, not an entrance upon genuine Christian life.

Through most of church history, however, the church has considered rebaptism one of the cardinal sins. The Donatists began the practice of rebaptism in the fourth century, and because their practice called into question the validity of

Catholic baptism, a Byzantine emperor imposed the death penalty for rebaptism. It was this ancient Justinian law that was invoked when the Anabaptists engaged in rebaptism a thousand years later at the time of the Reformation.

The question of rebaptism is not a mischievous question raised by Anabaptist troublemakers but arises out of the inherent nature of baptism as a sacrament. Since baptism is a rite with ordinary water that signifies grace and faith, we have before us the inescapable distinction between the sign and the thing signified and therefore the possibility of an empty sign without the reality it is supposed to signify. That is, it is possible to apply water in a formal ritual in which people are not really entering upon the way of faith. The question therefore arises: how does the church acknowledge or signify the fact when such people *do* truly come to faith later. A rather natural and logical suggestion would be to reapply the sign, this time in truth.

To rightly assess the problem of rebaptism we must remind ourselves of the basic meaning of the New Testament pattern. It is a sign of entrance upon the Christian way. In principle, then, there can and should be only one baptism, seeing there is only one beginning to the way of faith.

There can, of course, be a lapse from and a *return* to the Christian way. In the early church excommunicated penitents who returned to the church were received in a rite of absolution along with baptized catechumens at Easter. But the church did not rebaptize the lapsed who returned to faith, and neither should we.

A twofold difficulty presents itself in any attempt at a *real* (as compared to an only *apparent*) rebaptism. If the first baptism is real, marking actual entrance upon the Christian way, then the second is perforce empty, and to perform such a rebaptism is to endanger the integrity of the rite. If the first baptism is doubted, that tends to cast doubt upon the authenticity of the second as well. To put it another way, if there were a second real baptism, it would call the first real baptism into question and therewith also undermine itself. (A spurious first baptism can also, of course, foster doubts about the authenticity of a subsequent one.)

Because of the inherent meaning of baptism, a venture into the practice of rebaptism tends, therefore, to be self-defeating, not merely because it is unnecessary but because, strictly speaking, it is impossible. For this reason the church has always been justifiably touchy about rebaptism and has sought to avoid it.

But the question returns: what if an ostensible baptism is not an actual entrance upon the way of faith? Many churches who hold a sacramentalist view of baptism would like to deny that a spurious baptism can occur, for they claim that salvation is necessarily conferred in the very process of the rite. We hold that this sacramentalist claim cannot successfully be defended from either the Bible or experience.

It is worthy of note that the Catholic Church has not claimed infallibility in the rite of marriage, for some marriages are annulled. They are held in retrospect not to have been marriages. Hence, unlike divorced people who were considered really married and who cannot therefore remarry, people whose so-called marriages were annulled are free to marry. They do not, strictly speaking, remarry.

Similarly a baptism may be warranted (it is not a rebaptism, strictly speaking) where an earlier rite proved not to be a true baptism. A person should not be denied proper baptismal entrance upon the Christian way simply because that person or the church erred on a previous occasion. But such a baptism should be granted only if overwhelming clarity shows an earlier apparent baptism not to have been a true one. Like annulments of marriages, one would expect such instances to remain fairly uncommon—and to be handled with extreme care.

The problem, then, is not rebaptism. The problem is spurious baptism. And the answer is not an absolute refusal to rebaptize, which is to pretend that the church can never make a mistake, but rather to avoid hasty, premature, and indiscriminate baptisms. It is persistent acts of what is *called* baptism of people who are *not in fact* entering upon the way of faith that has the effect of eroding the credibility of the rite. The best solution to the so-called problem of rebaptism is conscientious care by the church to see to it that where the sign of baptism is applied it does indeed answer to the thing signified—that is, that baptism signifies the operation of the Spirit in evoking faith.

To sum up, the church has a right to be cautious about rebaptism. But the occurrence of an occasional instance of it has neither ruined the church nor eroded the integrity of the rite. The real danger has been the church's refusal to examine the reason for the rise of the demand for rebaptism. We should rather accept an occasional rebaptism than pretend infallibility and refuse to be honest about the real status of people with respect to faith.

With this review of the general principles governing the subject of rebaptism we can now take up the three kinds of situations that might arise in a congregation seeking a consistent believers baptism practice. We should carefully distinguish between the three different kinds.

Rebaptism of Persons Apparently Baptized as Believers

The first kind of situation is that of persons ostensibly baptized upon confession of faith who then claim, or about whom it is claimed, that their original baptism was not an authentic entrance upon the way of faith but only an empty ritual. Sometimes this takes place after a notable subsequent religious experience.

We have noted the need for caution on the part of the church in facing requests for rebaptism. If the church has satisfied itself that an ostensible first baptism was indeed not a genuine ownership of faith, then, as indicated in the foregoing, a baptism is warranted.

As also mentioned, however, the rise of the rebaptism issue should prompt the church to reexamine its baptismal practice in order to baptize with more care and integrity in the first place. The most common reason for the appearance of inclinations to seek rebaptism has been, at least in Mennonite churches, baptism of people who are too young. Sometimes mere children are pushed or cajoled into baptism, most often by their parents, before they have reached a sufficient measure of accountability to be able to make a real appropriation of the faith heritage in which they are being reared. Most problems concerning rebaptism would thus be taken care of if we took pains to respect the God-ordained pattern of how and when youth come to the age of discretion. We have too often heard young people say they were pushed into baptism prematurely and then later felt cheated out of the chance to be baptized at the point in their lives that actually marked their entrance upon a personally owned faith.

The legitimate concern for rebaptism just noted is to be distinguished from another kind of case, that of people who seek rebaptism because of a striking new religious experience, a sensational surge of faith and joy so phenomenal (at least to their feeling at the moment) that they desire to celebrate it in baptism.

It must be admitted that according to the New Testament

pattern baptism often is accompanied by the striking psychological concomitants just mentioned, though we also observed in an earlier chapter that these sensational experiences are not as likely to occur in the case of someone brought up in the community of faith. But because baptism is meant to mark a person's initial appropriation of the life of faith, we are not justified in employing this rite to celebrate subsequent experiences of growth in faith, no matter how sensational.

The hankering for rebaptism arises too often because in retrospect people consider their baptism to have been somewhat pallid. If so, the answer to the problem is, on the one hand, to refuse to adulate sensational conversions and, on the other hand, to celebrate adequately the less sensational but more excellent way of coming to faith through nurture within the community of faith. The church should strive to make the celebration of every baptism less routine, to invest the rite with all the rich meaning baptism possesses and to take the time to realize its import, as we noted in our discussion of the mode of baptism.

Rebaptism of Persons Baptized as Infants Upon Their Entrance to an Owned Faith

The believers church has not usually had any hesitation about baptizing those baptized in infancy who for some reason or other come to adolescence and the appropriation of the Christian heritage of faith in a believers church setting. The logic of this position has already been anticipated in the preceding chapters of this book, and we need not elaborate it at length here.

We have noted that the New Testament pattern of baptism of the adult convert from the non-Christian world does not directly fit children or youth of the church. Because the presence of responsible faith is the definitive mark of baptism in the New Testament model, we have argued that the best adaptation of that model is not to use it to receive infants but to mark appropriation of the faith by accountable adolescents or young adults. We have observed that the biblical heritage already supplies us with a rite for reception of infants. Moreover, using baptism to receive infants only necessitates the creation of another rite, confirmation, which can be called a surrogate baptism, to signify ownership of faith of persons at the age of accountability.

Since the believers church does not possess a rite of confirmation, but chiefly because it is convinced baptism applies where pedobaptists confirm, the believers church does not hesitate to baptize those who were baptized in infancy at that point where they appropriate the faith in adolescence. Believers baptism theology does not see this as a rebaptism any more than pedobaptists see confirmation as a rebaptism. The use of two rites in both pedobaptist and believers baptism traditions—one rite for infants and one for those owning the faith at the age of discretion—shows that they perform two quite different functions. The term rebaptism is therefore really inappropriate here.

For reasons similar to those just mentioned the believers church does not hesitate to baptize adult converts from the non-Christian world who were baptized in infancy but then became alienated for a season from the life of the church.

The believers church position and policy sketched here has been longstanding Anabaptist-Mennonite practice, and though it has tended to bother some pedobaptists, it is the most logically consistent position from a believers church standpoint. Moreover this position has sustained a consistent and healthy church life in line with the believers church vision. I see no reason for changing our position on this point.

Rebaptism of Persons at Transfer of Church Membership

We occasionally receive applications for membership in a believers church, perhaps because of marriage, of persons who were never baptized upon confession of faith but are at the time of their coming without doubt practicing Christians. In the past our churches often required baptism of such people, but recently many congregations have dropped this requirement.

On the cardinal principle that baptism signifies the act of accountable entrance upon the way of faith, we must decide that baptism is out of place here, for the individual in question is not now coming to faith but has been a practicing Christian for possibly many years and is merely transferring church membership.

In view of what baptism means, to impose baptism upon such an individual implies that he or she was not a Christian and is only now coming to faith. To misuse baptism in *this* fashion would be a serious perversion of its real meaning and could not but subvert the proper understanding and practice of baptism in general. If we say we are not implying a person's entrance upon the Christian way at the point of baptism, then we are inevitably distorting the meaning of baptism in another direction, implying that baptism confers some higher righteousness the believer in question does not yet supposedly possess.

If we wish to protect the integrity of baptism we do well to refrain from imposing it upon people to try to make up in the middle of their Christian life what we regard as a deficiency in their earlier church experience. The old saying applies here: two wrongs do not make a right.

To conclude, every congregation will likely need to make some decisions and judgments about rebaptism sooner or later, and when it does it will be best equipped for good discernment if it keeps in mind this one principle: Whether in the case of a convert from the non-Christian world or of someone nurtured in the church, we should as conscientiously as possible administer baptism at that point in time where God's grace moves persons to accountable undertaking of the Christian way.

Chapter 8

THE MORE EXCELLENT WAY

Owning the Heritage of Faith

I would venture to say that the line of thought we have taken in this book is not strange or disquieting to many readers. They have found themselves moving to a similar position, perhaps intuitively, whether or not they have found it adequately formulated somewhere. Other readers will find the thesis presented here new, unfamiliar, and perhaps even troubling.

The very appearance of this book implies that the position presented is not widely enough understood. It certainly was not understood through most of church history, and it is not sufficiently understood today. Moreover the implications of this position for congregational church life and practice are still usually not clear enough. Let us therefore review and summarize.

We do well to reemphasize before going any further that the New Testament pattern of baptism has never become obsolete. That pattern represents the adult convert entering the messianic community from the outside world, and it will remain a functioning pattern of baptism, used by all Christian denominations, as long as there remain non-Christian people in the world. Indeed, the statistics of recent studies in missions show the percentage of the world that is even formally Christian declining in the face of phenomenal world population growth, despite the exceptional growth of Christianity in some parts of the world such as sub-Sahara Africa.

So we can be assured that the New Testament pattern of the baptism of adult converts will be around yet for some time to come. The thesis of this book in no way depreciates this New Testament pattern when used in the right way at the right time and place. Long may the gospel show its power in bringing people from darkness to light and from the power of Satan to God (Acts 26:18), this crossover being signified in baptism.

Granting the validity of the New Testament model of baptism, we cannot escape the conviction that a problem exists in the application of the New Testament pattern when it comes to children of the church. Despite our protestations that God has no grandchildren, that all have sinned and fallen short of the glory of God, that all must be born of water and of the Spirit, the inescapable fact remains: the conversion and baptism of people in accord with the New Testament model creates—and is intended to create—a new situation. Their children cannot and should not need to grow up in a sinful environment but are privileged to grow up under the instruction and discipline of the Lord, to use once again the apostle's familiar cadences in Ephesians 6. And the better that parents and the church fulfill their task of instruction and discipling, the less likely or even possible it is for second-generation Christians to have the experience of conversion and baptism of their first-generation Christian parents. The experience of children in the church will instead be one of appropriation and ownership of the faith in which they have been brought up, even if that appropriation includes willing rejection of the non-Christian way, the renunciation of the devil and all his works.

As already suggested, the different situation of children of the church is not to be lamented but celebrated, because the object of the conversion and baptism of a first-generation Christian is precisely the creation of regenerated marriages, homes, and congregations that makes possible the nurture of children in the values of the Christian way. To be privileged to grow up within the community of faith and to own that faith when reaching the age of discretion, I call the more excellent way, borrowing Paul's expression in 1 Corinthians 13.

We don't need to disparage the conversion of first-generation Christians from the non-Christian world. Thank God for every one thus saved. But wonderful as it is to see sinners rescued from lives of sin, and justifiable as it may be to appreciate them as trophies of grace, to spare people any period of life in the service of sin is still God's preference. It still remains the more excellent way.

If the situation of children of the church is different from that of adult unbelievers, there are several possible ways of trying to relate the New Testament pattern of baptism. The church could, of course, decline altogether to require baptism of children of the church on the ground that they can be considered already fully Christian due to birth within the community of faith. We have seen, however, that the overwhelming majority of Christians through history and today have rejected this option.

The first way of trying to apply the New Testament pattern of baptism to children of the church is to require adolescents and post-adolescents to duplicate the New Testament pattern by passing through an interim of actual (or artifical?) sinfulness and rejection of faith in order to be able to experience an authentic (or again artificial?) repentance and conversion. This achieves a measure of external conformity with the New Testament pattern of an adult crossover from unbelief to faith and life in the Christian community. We reject this way of applying the New Testament model, however, both because we deplore the expectation that children of the church should spend any period of their lives in unfaith and because too many can be and are lost to the church permanently. The price is too high.

The second way of trying to apply the New Testament pattern of baptism to children of the church is to impose it upon them in the preadolescent, innocent period of life. On this view children who have not yet reached the age of discretion or accountability are considered culpable sinners who must be invited to repent and be converted from sin to righteousness.

We find this second way of applying the New Testament model problematic for several reasons. For one thing, it is a violation of the God-ordained innocence of children. For another, it is a contradiction in terms to expect a New Testament kind of accountable decision from not-yet-accountable children. Again, imposing an adult kind of conversion experience upon children creates the risk of serious confusion when they do reach the age of discretion. Then they either feel no need to appropriate the faith, assuming it was done at an earlier point of time; or they make an appropriation of their faith heritage but then have no way to signify it and therefore have doubts about its authenticity, both because of the absence of a signifying rite and because of the growing awareness of an earlier inauthentic rite.

Classic Catholic, Lutheran, and Anglican doctrine and practice carry this second way of applying the New Testament model of baptism to the extreme of infant baptism. That is, it presumes to make a direct application of the New Testament pattern of baptism of adult converts upon newborn children. It alleges that all that baptism means in the New Testament—repentance, regeneration, bestowal of the Spirit, discipleship, faith—this work of grace occurs at the baptism of an infant at the font, just as some Baptists contend that it happens in the baptistry to a child of five or seven years of age.

In Western Christianity today infant baptism is of course almost invariably followed by confirmation, indicating the development of another meaning in the baptism of children—a recognition of the privilege of birth or adoption into the covenant community and nurture within it. Baptism signifies commitment of the church to Christian nurture of such children. And such baptism is appropriately, even necessarily, followed by confirmation, at which the baptized children, when they come to the age of discretion, own the covenant in which they were reared.

This rationale for infant baptism has the merit of not only recognizing the special status of children of the church but also of respecting the meaning of the New Testament model of baptism and refusing to pretend to use it unchanged in the case of children. This rationale, originating chiefly in Calvinism but now prevailing far beyond historic Calvinist churches, frankly structures two orders of baptism, one for adult converts and one for children.

We have noted, though, the chief difficulties in this rationale. First, it constrains baptism to perform a function for which there already exists a biblical rite, infant dedication. Then, having thus transferred the function of baptism, it must create the new rite of confirmation, a surrogate baptism, to signify the ownership of covenant faith by youth of the church. Again, this third way draws an invidious contrast between children of believers and other children, not adequately accepting the innocence of all children and the responsibility of the church to fulfill its mission to all children of the world as far as this is possible.

We have argued for a third alternative, which incorporates the insights of the pedobaptist tradition and yet also preserves the fundamental meaning of the New Testament pattern of baptism. This alternative recognizes the innocence of all children—and our responsibility to them—as well as the privileged position of children of the church (not merely children of Christians but all children brought under the influence of Christian teaching and values). It recognizes the possibility and desirability of seeking to move children from innocence to the Christian way in adolescence. Our alternative argues for the appropriateness of baptism at this point as a sign of their crossing-over from innocence into an owned faith, signifying their identification with and appropriation of the heritage reaching back through Jesus of Nazareth to the exodus.

Such baptism signifies that one is not a member of the body of Christ, the messianic community, simply as a result of natural birth, but as a consequence of responsible faith. At the same time such baptism concedes that those who have adopted the life of the redeemed community can bring its grace to bear upon the task of nurturing children, giving them the benefit of a total life under the blessings of the kingdom of God. This is the privilege of those who believe that the messianic age has dawned and that we may—and must—take up in the present age the life of the age to come.

This pattern of baptism for youth of the church as sketched in this book must frankly be conceded as an adaptation of the New Testament model. But it possesses the merit of remaining closest to the principles of the New Testament pattern in that accountable ownership of faith remains the central act signified by the application of water. Second-generation Christians need not return to Egyptian bondage. They are privileged to grow up in the promised land of the community of faith. But they must appropriate for themselves the spiritual life they were taught and had modeled for them as a consequence of the crossing over of their forebears. And if that act of appropriating covenant faith is to be signified with a rite called water baptism, that rite is applied most fittingly at the point where such appropriation actually occurs.

Let us conclude by outlining briefly some do's and don'ts of an authentic practice of baptism with children and youth of the church.

1. Do practice dedication of infants or children. Develop, or continue to use, a service in line with the rich biblical practice of receiving children with thanks as a gift of God, recognizing them to be his, and accepting our task as parents and church to be stewards of our children, responsible to bring them up in the instruction and discipline of the Lord. God has privileged them to be placed by birth within the environment of faith.

2. Do commit yourself to diligent religious education. Develop skills in parenting through workshops and personal study. Then do not neglect to give Christian instruction in the home. Also put yourself behind a really excellent program of religious education in your congregation. Such instruction should, of course, be made appropriate to the respective ages of children.

As they are growing up, children of the church should be getting a sharpened sense of the people of God as an option and why it makes sense to take that option. Above all, be an example of the faith you are trying to teach.

3. Do try to minister to any and all the children in the world you can reach, using tact and wisdom. Such outreach includes communicating knowledge of the Bible story, Christian attitudes, and moral values. It involves especially the building of relationships.

Try in your congregation and neighborhood to bring as many children as possible under the influence of the Christian way. Make the Christian way an appealing way, presenting itself as a natural and desirable way to human joy, peace, and hope—which is what it is.

4. Do respect the innocence of preadolescent children. Do not treat them like adult sinners and generate harmful guilt feelings in them. Do not ask them to do what only persons who have reached the age of discretion can do, that is, make an accountable decision to take up the Christian way with all that that entails.

Do, however, honor the religion of childhood—that is, childhood expressions of understanding of the faith and childhood responses to its claims. Accept their childhood understanding of God and his love as God does. Accept their childhood expressions of prayer to God and love for Jesus. But as you would distinguish between children playing wedding and the real marriage of young adults, so also distinguish the religion of innocence from accountable faith.

5. Do take seriously your ministry to adolescents and newly independent young adults. Give special attention to the challenges and opportunities emerging at this transition in life. Do not assume that adolescents must move into a period of estrangement from the church. Such an expectation is easily discerned—and fulfilled—by your young people.

Do not treat adolescent youth and young adults as though they are excused somehow from making a real decision about faith. To make no decision is to make a decision, the decision *not* to identify with the Christian way. The decision to take the Christian way should be held up as the most desirable, worthwhile, logical, and even natural thing one could do. Be sure to preserve a balance between urgent invitation and patient respect for an honest decision.

6. Do hold meaningful baptisms. Do not merely surrender five or ten minutes out of the morning service for this event, but take time to celebrate, as you do at a wedding, the momentous transition baptism represents in the life of one or several of your people. Do not structure the service of baptism as a family or clan ritual. Expect the congregation to participate, since this is an act of the family of God. For persons to espouse the Christian way is, after all, what the church is all about.

Do not process candidates in annual baptismal classes. Avoid annual classes the way you would avoid once-a-year weddings. Instead, schedule baptisms when accountable appropriation of the Christian way is discerned in individuals. That may involve one or more youth at any time of the year.

Do make baptism a Christian service, the focus of which is making a covenant. Remember that it is a *church* rite, not a youth social. Central to the service of baptism is the act of confession of faith, when youth of the church own the faith of the community that nurtured them.

7. Do involve young people in the life of the church following their baptism. Give them the kind of support and recognition befitting the importance of their step of faith. Make baptism not the *end* of a period of instruction, but the beginning of lifelong discipleship in the church. Involve newly baptized youth in the giving and receiving of

counsel. Include them in the work of the church. Acknowledgment of the significance of their crossover into an owned covenant life makes for assurance, growth, and confidence in service in the community of faith.

Baptism according to the New Testament is God's provision for people to cross over from bondage to the community of faith. The establishment of a community of faith through baptism then creates the opportunity for nurture within the way of faith and eventual personal appropriation of this faith by those nurtured in it. Let us embrace this God-ordained economy of salvation and work with him in the more excellent way.

Notes

1. Rollin Stely Armour, *Anabaptist Baptism* (Herald Press, Scottdale, Pa., 1966). Henry Poettcker, *A Study on Baptism* (Faith and Life Press, Newton, Kan., 1963).

2. Karl Barth, *The Teaching of the Church Regarding Baptism* (SCM Press, London, 1948).

3. Most useful are the reviews of infant baptism by Joachim Jeremias, *Infant Baptism in the First Four Centuries*, SCM Press, London, 1960; and *The Origins of Infant Baptism*, SCM Press, London, 1963; Kurt Aland, *Did the Early Church Baptize Infants?* Westminster Press, Philadelphia, 1963. Jeremias says the early church did, Aland says it did not, practice infant baptism, though both endorse infant baptism today. Also useful is a trio of books by British Baptists: A. Gilmore, ed., *Christian Baptism*, The Judson Press, Valley Forge, 1959; R. E. O. White, *The Biblical Doctrine of Initiation*, Eerdmans, Grand Rapids, 1960s; and G. R. Beasley-Murray, *Baptism in the New Testament*, Eerdmans, 1973.

4. *Encyclopedia Judaica*, Macmillan, New York, 1971, article on "Proselyte."

5. *Ibid.*

6. White, pp. 61, 65, 66.

7. *Hasting's Encyclopedia of Religion and Ethics*, Scribners, New York, 1955, article on "Baptism."

8. White, p. 68.

9. *Gospel Parallels*, ed. Burton H. Throckmorton, Jr., Thomas Nelson and Sons, New York, 1949, 1957, p. 10.

10. Gilmore, p. 115.

11. *The Englishman's Greek Concordance of the New Testament*, Samuel Bagster and Sons, London, 1903.

12. Beasley-Murray, p. 298.

13. Beasley-Murray, p. 282.

14. White, p. 165.

15. "Many Free Churchmen have lost all sense of baptism as entry into membership of the Church and would be surprised (sic) at the suggestion that it should be so regarded. Even Baptists in Britain not infrequently baptize young people on profession of faith without raising the question of Church membership (though that is a fall from Baptist theology rather than an expression of it). The Churches need to be delivered from careless practice, for theoretically they know better than what they do." Beasley-Murray, p. 282.

16. White, p. 181.

17. I have discussed this subject more fully in my *Discipling the Brother*, Herald Press, Scottdale, 1972, chapter 8, "The Wheat and the Tares: The Visibility of the Church," and so I refer the interested reader to that book.

18. Oscar Cullmann, *Baptism in the New Testament*, SCM Press, London, 1950, pp. 71ff.

19. John Frederick Jansen, *The Meaning of Baptism*, Westminster Press, Philadelphia, 1958, p. 59.

20. Geoffrey Wainwright, *Christian Initiation*, John Knox Press, Richmond, 1969, p. 11.

21. Johannes Warns, *Studies in the Original Christian Baptism*, Kregel Publications, Grand Rapids, 1958, pp. 87-91.

22. *Ibid.*

23. Gilmore, p. 211, and Jeremias, *Infant Baptism in the First Four Centuries*, p. 95.

24. Beasley-Murray, p. 366.

25. Royal F. Peterson, *Baptized into Christ*, Augustana Press, Rock Island, 1959, pp. 24, 27.

26. Warns, p. 83.

27. John Horsch, *Infant Baptism*, Scottdale, 1917, p. 47. Horsch

quotes from a Hutterite document called "Reply to Colman Rorer" that has never been published but that Horsch read at a Hutterite Colony in Canada.

28. In a letter to John Knox, according to Beasley-Murray, p. 348.

29. *Institutes of the Christian Religion*, Book IV, Chapter XV, 22.

30. G. W. Bromiley, *Baptism and the Anglican Reformers*, Lutterworth Press, London, 1953, p. 110.

31. See, for example, Dom Gregory Dix, *The Theology of Confirmation in Relation to Baptism*, Dacre Press, London, 1946; and Burkhard Neunheuser, OSB, *Baptism and Confirmation*, Herder and Herder, New York, 1964.

32. Paul K. Jewett, *Infant Baptism and the Covenant of Grace*, Eerdmans, Grand Rapids, 1978, pp. 193-207.

33. Beasley-Murray, p. 348.

34. W. F. Flemington, *The New Testament Doctrine of Baptism*, SPCK, London, 1953, pp. 82ff.

35. Cullmann, p. 28, referring to the view of F. Leenhardt in "Le baptême chrétien," Cahiers théologiques de l'Actualité protestante, No. 4, 1944, p. 69.

36. Quoted from the same Leenhardt article by Beasley-Murray, p. 374.

37. James Fowler, *Stages of Faith*, Harper and Row, San Francisco, 1981; and John H. Westerhoff, *Will Our Children Have Faith?* Seabury Press, New York, 1976.

38. See Paul Lederach, *The Spiritual Family and the Biological Family*, Herald Press, Scottdale, 1973.

39. Gideon Yoder, The Nurture and Evangelism of Children, Herald Press, Scottdale, 1959, pp. 80ff.

40. *Webster's New Collegiate Dictionary*, 7th Edition.

41. Westerhoff, pp. 89-103.

42. Martin Marty, *Baptism*, Fortress Press, Philadelphia, 1962, p. 18.

43. Stephen J. England, *The One Baptism*, The Bethany Press, St. Louis, 1960, p. 88.

44. Gilmore, p. 209.

45. In his anti-Anabaptist bias Calvin denies that a baptism in water took place in the incident reported in Acts 19. Paul merely

laid (dry) hands upon these disciples to confer the Holy Spirit, says Calvin. *Institutes*, Book IV, Chapter XV, 18.

Select Bibliography

Aland, Kurt. *Did the Early Church Baptize Infants?* Westminster Press, Philadelphia, 1953. Aland says it didn't, even though as a modern Lutheran he endorses infant baptism.

Armour, Rollin Stely. *Anabaptist Baptism*, Herald Press, Scottdale, 1966. A dissertation on the views concerning baptism in Hubmaier, Hut, Hofmann, and Marpeck.

Barth, Karl. *The Teaching of the Church Regarding Baptism*, SCM Press, London, 1948. A small but explosive publication in which Barth declares himself for believers baptism.

Beasley-Murray, G. R. *Baptism in the New Testament*, Eerdmans, Grand Rapids, 1962. The best general study of baptism in the New Testament; it also devotes a chapter to baptism in church history.

Bridge, Donald, and Phypers, David. *The Water that Divides*, InterVarsity Press, Leicester, 1977. Two British evangelicals dialogue across the pedobaptism/believers baptism divide.

Cullman, Oscar. *Baptism in the New Testament*, SCM Press, London, 1950. A reaffirmation of infant baptism, contra Barth.

Dix, Dom Gregory. *The Theology of Confirmation in Relation to Baptism*, Dacre Press, London, 1946. A short essay that struggles with the problem of the separation between baptism and confirmation in Western Christianity.

Flemington, W. F. *The New Testament Doctrine of Baptism*, SPCK, London, 1953. A moderate British Methodist voice on baptism in the New Testament.

Funk, Henry. *A Mirror of Baptism*. The first German edition, 1744. The last English one, 1890, John Baer's Sons, Lancaster. A statement of the classic Mennonite doctrine of three baptisms, the baptisms of water, Spirit, and blood.

Gilmore, A., ed., *Christian Baptism*, Judson Press, Philadelphia, 1959. Essays by British Baptists covering the whole history of baptism.

Jeremias, Joachim. *Infant Baptism in the First Four Centuries*, SCM Press, London, 1960. The argument is that infant baptism was practiced in the earliest church.

Jewett, Paul K. *Infant Baptism and the Covenant of Grace*, Eerdmans, Grand Rapids, 1978. A Fuller Theological Seminary professor argues for "believer baptism" not in spite of but because of Calvinist covenant theology.

Marcel, Pierre Ch. *The Biblical Doctrine of Infant Baptism*, James Clarke and Company, London, 1953. A French Reformed pastor's zealous argument for infant baptism.

Moody, Dale. *Baptism: Foundation for Christian Unity*, Westminster Press, 1967. A Southern Baptist (Louisville) professor reviews very objectively the Reformed, Lutheran, Anglican, and Free Church positions on baptism.

Poettcker, Henry. *A Study on Baptism*, Faith and Life Press, Newton, 1963. A Mennonite New Testament scholar's reading of biblical teaching on baptism.

Wainwright, Geoffrey. *Christian Initiation*, John Knox Press, Richmond, 1969. An irenic survey of the main biblical, historical, and contemporary theological issues in the ecumenical dialogue on baptism.

Warns, Johannes. *Baptism*, Kregel Publications, Grand Rapids, 1958. A German Baptist argument against infant baptism.

Westerhoff, John H. *Will Our Children Have Faith?* Seabury, New York, 1976. Some very basic and important observations about the faith development of children.

White, R. E. O. *The Biblical Doctrine of Initiation*, Eerdmans, Grand Rapids, 1960. A thorough and systematic study by a British Baptist on baptism in the New Testament.

Yoder, Gideon. *The Nurture and Evangelism of Children,* Herald Press, Scottdale, 1959. An attempt to work toward healthy Christian principles in our ministry to children, though the book does not delineate implications for baptismal practice.

A native of Saskatchewan, Canada, **Marlin Jeschke** received his BA from Tabor College, Hillsboro, Kansas, his divinity degree from Garrett-Evangelical Seminary, and his PhD in theology from Northwestern University, Evanston, Illinois.

He has taught in the religion department at Goshen College since 1961, and is presently professor of Philosophy and Religion there and chairman of the Division of Bible, Religion, and Philosophy.

He grew up in a Mennonite church, receiving baptism at the age of eighteen. Currently he is a member of the College Mennonite Church in Goshen, Indiana. He is married, and he and his wife, Charmaine, have three children.